THE BEST MAN'S HANDBOOK
A Guy's Guide to the Big Event

by James Grace

Illustrated by David McGrievey

RUNNING PRESS
PHILADELPHIA · LONDON

Text © 1999 by James Grace
Illustrations © 1999 by David McGrievey
All rights reserved under the Pan-American and International Copyright Conventions
Printed in the United States

9   8   7   6   5   4   3
Digit on the right indicates the number of this printing

Library of Congress Cataloging-in-Publication Number 98-66653
ISBN 0-7624-0499-X

Cover and interior design by Terry Peterson
Typography: Monotype Bembo and ITC Stone Sans

This book may be ordered by mail from the publisher.
Please include $2.50 for postage and handling.
But try your bookstore first!

Running Press Book Publishers
125 South Twenty-second Street
Philadelphia, Pennsylvania 19103-4399

Visit us on the web!
www.runningpress.com

Dedication

This book is dedicated to my wife, Lisa,
for her unending love and support.

Contents

Introduction

WHY YOU NEED TO READ THIS BOOK

YOU, THE BEST MAN OR GROOMSMAN, HAVE AGREED TO TAKE part in a friend's or relative's wedding in a unique and rewarding manner. You have agreed to stand up in public with another man and support him in his decision to marry. At this point, you may have come to the realization that you have no idea what you're doing. Fear not, because from this point forward, the collective wisdom of many men—some wise, some not—will be with you.

So You Think You're Up to the "Job"?

As a Best Man or Groomsman, you'll play an important role in the wedding process. Failure to perform your functions could spell disaster for the Groom and Bride and place your well-being in jeopardy. In the age of videographers and disposable cameras, any blunders, miscalculations, or oversights could be recorded for posterity and become the stuff of wedding legend. These could simultaneously eliminate any chance you may have of running for political office and exponentially increase your chance of being a guest on *America's Funniest Home Videos*. For these and many other reasons, take no chances: apply the Best Man's philosophy, mission, and goals. If you do, you'll be the envy of your peers, respected by children, and an honored member of the Groom and Bride's inner circle for many years to come.

Why I Wrote This Book

How did this book come to be, you may ask? At a wedding I attended, the Best Man made a confession during his speech: He stated that he had no idea what he was doing when he accepted the "job" of Best Man. He explained how he searched for sage advice among the normal caches of wisdom—bookstores, the Internet, and his family and friends. He discovered that while a plethora of information exists for the Bride and Maid of Honor, there remains little to be found for the Best Man or Groomsmen.

As I pondered his observations, it struck me that all this information exists for those members of the wedding process who already have a good idea about what they're doing. Think of it this way—if you were to place a bet on any person associated with the process who had the most potential for completely screwing up a good wedding, you'd have to go with the Best Man, before even considering the other Groomsmen. Now, to think that this group, with the most potential for disaster, is also the group that is the least informed. I'm no genius, but it doesn't take one to see how scary this situation is. (If the Bride had time to think about it, she'd probably realize her sudden weight loss over the few months prior to the wedding—termed by those in the know as "Skinny Bride's Syndrome"—is the result of a subconscious realization of this risk.)

This observation was like a bolt of lightning to me. I wrote the idea on a napkin before I forgot it—I told you I'm no genius—because I knew I had a duty not to let another man down. The book you now hold is the result.

Initially I thought that I could write the entire book based on my own observations and experiences. I thought my involvement in many weddings, including the planning of my own, provided me with enough to offer on this subject. I soon discovered, however, that there exist very few definitive answers to many of the "big" Best Man or Groomsmen questions. I realized I would be doing men a disservice if I only included my ideas and experiences and not those of other men and women who have gone through this process.

To solve this problem, I created and disseminated the survey that appears on the following pages. Many men and women shared their stories, insights, and warnings. Please take the time to complete the survey before you continue, because your answers will help you understand your initial ideas and impressions. When you finish reading the book, go back and see what ideas have changed or have been strengthened based on what you've read.

THE BEST MAN AND GROOMSMEN SURVEY

I. INTRODUCTION

a) You are? _____ Male _____ Female
   Married? _____ (Yes) _____ (No)   Age? _____
b) What is approximate number of weddings you have attended? _____
c) How many times have you been a Best Man? _____
d) How many times have you been in a wedding party? _____
e) How many bachelor parties have you attended? _____

II. THE BACHELOR PARTY

a) Do you enjoy bachelor parties? _____ (Yes) _____ (No)
   Please explain your answer.

b) In your opinion, what is the purpose of the bachelor party?

c) Rate each of these elements of a bachelor party.
   (1 = Very important to 5 = Not important)

_____ Male friends   _____ Activities (sports, pool, darts, etc.)
_____ Food   _____ Gambling
_____ Safe Transportation   _____ Cigars
_____ Adult Entertainment   _____ Alcohol
_____ Coed Guests   _____ Music
_____ Other (please list and explain)   _____

d) What are some of the best and/or worst ideas for bachelor parties
of which you have heard or taken part?

e) Should the Groom and/or the Bride have a say in the planning of the bachelor party, including whether there should be adult entertainment?
Groom _____ (Yes) _____ (No)   Bride _____ (Yes) _____ (No)

Who should have a say? Please explain your answer.

Please answer questions f, h, and i with a dollar range.

f) What is a reasonable amount for each Groomsman to spend for hosting a bachelor party? _____

g) Do you think the Best Man should spend an equal, greater, or lesser amount than the Groomsmen?
_____ (equal) _____ (greater) _____ (lesser) What normally occurs?_____

h) What is a reasonable amount for guests to spend at a bachelor party?

_____

i) What is a reasonable amount for transportation? _____

j) What different types of transportation have you seen provided at bachelor parties?

III. THE REHEARSAL DINNER
a) From your experience, how often are the Best Man and/or Grooms-men asked to speak at the rehearsal dinner?
Best Man: _____ Never _____ Rarely_____ Sometimes
_____ Often _____ Always

Groomsmen: _____ Never _____ Rarely_____ Sometimes
_____ Often _____ Always

b) What's a good thing to say at a rehearsal dinner? How should it differ from the wedding toast?

IV. THE SPEECH

a) What are the elements of a good Best Man speech?

b) How long should the Best Man speech be? (Please check the appropriate choice.)

_____ Less than one minute   _____ One to five minutes
_____ Five to ten minutes   _____ Ten to fifteen minutes
_____ Greater than fifteen minutes
_____ Other_____

c) Rate each of these elements of a Best Man speech.
   (1 = Very important to 5 = Not important)

( ) Funny
( ) Sincere
( ) A good story about the Groom
( ) Audible
( ) An explanation of how the couple met
( ) A good ending toast
( ) How he has changed for the better since they met
( ) An explanation of how the Best Man and the Groom met
( ) Best Man is sober while giving the speech
( ) Other_____

d) What is the best or worst speech you have heard (i.e., a speech that was either fantastic or completely inappropriate)?

e) What is the best or worst toast you have heard (the final part of the speech where the Best Man and the guests raise their glasses to the couple)?

f) Have you been to a wedding where the Maid of Honor also gave a speech?
_____ (Yes) _____ (No)
   Please describe.

V. THE WEDDING
a) What are some mistakes you have seen the Best Man or Groomsmen make at or before a wedding (i.e., with the ring, with the Bride, with the families, when a Groom no-showed, dancing faux pas, garter belt issues, during the "after-hours party," etc.)?

b) Do you have any tips for ushering? What works and what doesn't work?

c) As a member of a wedding party, how many times have you "met" someone at a wedding? _____

d) Please share any 1) good stories 2) introductory lines or overall approaches.

e) Any last words of wisdom for a Best Man or Groomsmen to be?

Chapter 1

PREGAME WARM-UPS

NOW THAT YOU'VE COMPLETED THE SURVEY, YOU'RE READY to start "Best Man Bootcamp." You may have already begun to think about the bachelor party, your speech, or the overall type of Best Man or Groomsman you want to be. This chapter will provide you with a solid foundation on which to build. Nothing can replace real-world experience, but I believe that with this knowledge you'll someday venture forth and become the best Best Man and Groomsman you always wanted to be. Now fall out soldier—and make us all proud!

Philosophy

There will be times during the wedding process when you'll feel clueless. Don't worry, because the collective wisdom of the many contributors to this guide will be with you if you simply remember to use your common sense and apply the guide's general philosophy:

The wedding process isn't a time for the Best Man or the Groomsmen to shine. This is the Bride and Groom's event! You were asked only to share it with them and support them in making it a success.

This credo is often difficult for some members of the wedding to apply, but it's important that you recognize it and never forget it.

Mission

Any good mission should be simple to be effective. This guide's mission is the following:

Remain modest and calm, but always engaged.

This isn't your day, and most of the attention should be saved for 1) the Bride; 2) the Bride; 3) the Groom; 4) the Bride's family; 5) the Groom's family; 6) the wedding party; and 7) everyone else.

The Ten Goals of Highly Effective Best Men

To fulfill your mission you must also learn, internalize, and apply the following Best Man goals. What goals could there be, you may ask, beyond returning the tuxedo on time?

Gentlemen, please repeat after me . . .

1. I will not completely destroy the wedding, nor will I allow the other Groomsmen to completely destroy the wedding.
2. I will organize a great bachelor party that won't destroy the wedding or result in injury to any guests or paid entertainers.
3. I will prevent the survival of any tangible proof that the bachelor party actually took place.
(Please refer to Goals #1 and #2.)
4. I will ensure the Groom's attendance and successful completion of the wedding ceremony.
5. I will ensure that the Groom is sober and functional at the reception.
6. I will give a good speech that makes at least one person misty-eyed or prompts at least one guest over the age of 70 to utter the phrase: "Oh dear, wasn't that nice?"
7. I will out-do the Maid of Honor and the Bridesmaids at every juncture of the wedding while remaining an example to children.
8. I will, if "single," meet someone new at the wedding.
9. I will, if "happily single," not fall prey to the wedding/relationship gravitational pull.
10. I will eat and drink in moderation until the completion of my duties. (See Goals #1 through 9.)

These goals may appear overly simple or obvious at this point. But in practice it's this simplicity of judgment that usually gets lost, so don't get cocky. You have to trust the collective experience of the many who assisted in the development of these goals. The ability to apply these goals will become increasingly difficult throughout the wedding process. This will be the time when you'll be tested and ultimately judged on your abilities. Remember the mission: Remain modest and calm, but always engaged.

Pre-Wedding Events: How You Can Help

It's important to have an understanding of the overall wedding process. Once the question "Will you marry me?" is uttered, the Bride and Groom will have dozens of decisions to make during the months of their engagement. The first and most important decision will be to choose the location of the ceremony and reception. This decision affects the size and type of their wedding. The Bride and Groom must then decide on invitations, flowers, music, table settings, foods, drinks, color schemes, guest lists, officiators, gift registries, and the members of the wedding party.

Picking the wedding party can be one of the most difficult decisions because there never are enough spaces for every person the couple wants involved in the wedding. Many Grooms and Brides begin the task by asking their siblings and/or other relatives before adding a sampling of the friends they have collected over the course of their lives. There are no definite rules, but most often there will be an equal number of Groomsmen and Bridesmaids.

Once you're asked to be in the wedding, it's a nice gesture to send a thank-you note to the Bride and Groom that expresses how honored and excited you are about being a part of their wedding. If you wish, you can also offer your assistance during the wedding planning process. It would be very uncommon for them to ask you for help, but it's still a nice gesture.

There is one role that you can play during the wedding planning process—the role of confidant and sounding board. It's a good idea to check in with the Groom on a regular basis and see how he's holding up. This can be a stressful time, depending on the temperament of the people involved and the number of issues. The Groom may just need to talk with someone who knows the players but isn't actually involved in the process. This may sound like nothing, but it can be a valuable asset. If the Groom can keep his perspective and not take out his frustration on his Bride or other family members, it can only help the process. Don't be surprised if the Groom is at first reluctant to speak to you about any problems. Many people, once they get engaged, are reluctant to share anything negative for fear that it may reflect on the strength of their relationship. Just keep up the contact and let the Groom know that what he tells you will go no further.

If you don't live near the Groom, these phone calls may be your only contact with him during the months prior to his wedding. If you make an effort to stay in touch with him during this time, you'll feel more a part of the wedding even if you aren't available to assist him in other ways.

The Engagement Party
The engagement party is a fun event that can consist of anything from a small cook-out with close family and friends to a foreshadowing of the wedding reception with all the hoopla of a big dinner, slide shows, and speeches. Many Brides and Grooms don't get around to officially choosing their wedding party until after the engagement party. Even if they have picked you, you'll have very few obligations as a Best Man or Groomsman beyond those of any close friend. Just enjoy the party and try to meet as many people as you can, because many of them will be attending the bachelor party, rehearsal dinner, and wedding. First impressions are important; keep that in mind during this event.

The Bridal Shower
This event will be a women-only party 95% of the time. The Groom may be invited, but if you have any say in this, encourage him to politely

but firmly decline the invitation. The purpose of this event is to allow time for friends of the Bride, her mother, and the Groom's mother to get acquainted with one another. The Bride may be invited to more than one bridal shower, depending on her family.

The Bachelorette Party

This is another pre-wedding event, a more recent tradition. It often follows the bridal shower, and will involve the Bride's inner circle of female friends taking her out for one last night of raising Cain. As with the bachelor party, which we'll talk about later, the watchword is the same: silence. Remember: What goes around comes around.

The Jack and Jill Party

There exists one more type of pre-wedding event called a Jack and Jill Party. This is a co-ed party, that is a hybrid of an engagement party and a bridal shower. These parties can be entertaining if some events are planned beyond just watching the Bride and Groom open gifts to the peanut gallery's forced "oohs" and "aahs."

The Tuxedo

Many Best Men and Groomsmen have questions about the tuxedo rental process. But it isn't a given anymore that the Bride and Groom will ask you to wear a tux. If they choose not to have tuxes, they should either give you clear instructions as to what to wear or rent the outfit for you.

If the Bride and Groom choose to have a tux, the rental process is very easy. Most of the work is done for you. Normally, the Bride and Groom will choose a tux rental shop near the Groom's house and, with the help of the store employees, select the right tux for their wedding.

It isn't up to you to pick or comment on the style, color, or shoes selected. The Bride and Groom then provide the shop with the names of the people renting tuxes for their wedding.

Your job is twofold. First, you must get your tux measurements to the store within a week of the wedding. Any tux rental store, not just the store used by the Bride and Groom, will take your measurements and send them to the store chosen by the Bride and Groom. This is

great for those people who live out of state and don't want to wait until they are in town to deal with the tux. Most stores charge a fee of between $10 and $15 for this service. Second, your job is to pick up your tux within a few days of the wedding and not lose it. The store will request that you try the tux on while in the shop, so take that time to see that it fits properly and that all the appropriate extras are attached.

How to Tie a Bow Tie

1

Start with end in left hand extending 1" below that in right hand.

2

Cross longer end over shorter end and pass up through loop.

3

Form front loop of bow by doubling up shorter (hanging) end and placing it across collar points.

4

Hold front loop with thumb and forefinger of left hand. Drop longer end down over front of bow.

5

Place right forefinger, pointing up, on bottom half of hanging part. Pass up behind front loop.

6

Poke resulting loop through knot behind front loop. Even the ends and tighten.

Introduction to the Wonderful World of Sidebars

What is a sidebar? Why have them? And what's with the TIPS?

You'll see throughout the book extra text not included in the body of the page, but separated for your viewing convenience. Why? Because there's nothing like a sidebar to bring out a real pearl of wisdom. Some of these sidebars will be called TIPS. I've placed a minimum dollar value on each TIP to let you know its intrinsic value. The value of the TIPS alone are worth more than $40.00. At that price, even if you only use half of the TIPS, you're still getting a bargain with this book!

Chapter 2

THE BACHELOR PARTY

T HE BACHELOR PARTY, THAT STRANGE BLEND OF CIRCUS SIDE-show and wake, is one of the Best Man and Groomsmen's major responsibilities. The positive idea driving this event is the good fellowship gained by bringing together the Groom and Bride's male inner circle prior to the wedding ceremony. The underbelly of this event has some legitimate potholes that can and have negatively affected more than their share of weddings. The purpose of this chapter is to help you organize a successful event by exposing the many different aspects of a bachelor party. To this end, I've included some discussions on important topics that may arise during the planning process, such as evaluating your planning team, transportation, fundraising, costs, and party ideas.

Where Did the Concept "Best Man" Come From?

According to *The Book of Answers* by Barbara Berliner with Melinda Corey and George Ochoa, the term "Best Man" comes from Scotland, where it was rooted in the tradition of the Bridegroom simply kidnapping the woman he wanted as his Bride. The Groom would enlist his friends to help him, and the toughest and bravest of these "Groomsmen" would be the Best Man.

The Goal of the Bachelor Party

Once again you need to understand the goal before you undertake any worthwhile event. The goal of the bachelor party is simple:

To gather the various men from the Groom's and Bride's lives and blend them together in an entertaining, engaging, and safe event.

What Men Really Think About Bachelor Parties

It may seem a strange issue to address at such an early point in this chapter. Of course men like bachelor parties—why else would almost every Best Man and Groomsman help organize one for the Groom? But it turns out that although many men indicated that they like bachelor parties when they're done well, many more voiced their dislikes. It's important to understand these concerns before you can begin to organize a successful event. First, go back and see what you wrote in the survey. Your thoughts about bachelor parties will be important as you begin to make plans with the Groom or his other Groomsmen, because they may not all share the same sentiments.

I personally like bachelor parties if the organizers put some thought into the event. The truth is that I've participated in too many "Let's-get-the-Groom-drunk-on-horrid-shots-and-watch-him-do-the-Technicolor-yawn" nights to wish that on anyone. I've also been involved in many successful events where the guests enjoyed a good sense of fellowship that spilled over into the wedding day.

Don't get me wrong: I'm not necessarily challenging the custom that the Groom be drunk by the end of the night. That is a personal choice. Instead, I'm referring to how the other guests enjoy the night as this ritual takes place. A bachelor party is always better when the Best

Man attempts to include the whole group and not just the Groom. Including as many people as possible is very important because one purpose of the bachelor party is to create connections for people invited to the wedding which carry over to the actual wedding day and beyond.

The most enjoyable weddings are always the ones where you know the most people and when you have a connection to the group as a whole. It's amazing how many times you'll say to a friend, "You know [insert name here], he was at the bachelor party/wedding," as a way to connect different people from your life.

What Do the Men Say?

Not surprisingly, most of the men surveyed like bachelor parties. It isn't because of the strip bars or the alcohol, however. Rather, men like bachelor parties because of the camaraderie.

Here's a sampling of the responses I received:

"They're fun and usually a good excuse to get the gang back together."

"I'm not a fan of strip bars and most bachelor parties end up there. . . . Someone always regrets the evening."

"The bachelor party is, for many outside the Bride's and Groom's inner circle, the last party before the big wedding day. It's the last time to gather the troops and make one last stand against adulthood and responsibility."

"I enjoy them, but as I grow older I find I'm a little more uncomfortable with each one and I enjoy them less."

"It depends, because if tastefully done (i.e., minimal embarrassment for the Groom and the rest of the attendees, and no forced submission to sometimes heinous acts of exhibitionism), they can be a blast."

"I like every party."

"At first it was the mystique of attending a bachelor party, and now it's enjoyable as an evening to get together with 20 or 30 guys."

"I appreciate smaller intimate gatherings with close friends more and not fraternity parties and drunken endeavors."

"I enjoy bachelor parties because they are one of the last, great American all-male traditions."

One male respondent best summed up the bottom line of bachelor parties:

"Whether I like a bachelor party or not is absolutely dependent upon my relationship to Groom and the 'quality' of party. For example, I had the misfortune of attending a bachelor party for a guy I barely knew. . . . The 'party' consisted of about 75 middle-aged sidekicks who spent the smoke-filled evening reminiscing about those kooky, wild days of yesteryear while playing cards at make-shift gambling tables. On the other hand, a handful of close friends who get together to yack about the kooky, wild days of yesteryear could constitute a great evening."

One woman's view of the goal of a bachelor party:
"For men to get together and be, well, men by whatever definition they want."

What Is the Purpose of the Bachelor Party?

The purpose of the bachelor party is to build good relationships during a fun and entertaining event. What I discovered from the surveys and my own writing was a real inconsistency between the first answers, about whether men like bachelor parties, and what they thought its purpose was.

These particular survey responses sum up the pattern I saw:

Question 1. Do you enjoy bachelor parties?
"While it is often a good time to talk and drink with people you rarely see, most people who go to bachelor parties feel the need to drink to excess because it is the only time they get out with the guys. Also, there's far too much emphasis on whether there will be strippers at these parties."

Question 2. In your opinion, what is the purpose of the bachelor party?
"The purpose of the bachelor party is to give the future Groom a night of expected debauchery with the blessing of his fiancée. While this tends to contradict my previous editorial comments, I do think the bachelor party is a needed ritual to ensure the future Groom isn't completely lame."

How can you plan a party without knowing what people expect to be the result? It was interesting to hear from men who admitted their dislike for the idiocy and excesses of the bachelor party in the first question, then unequivocally stated that the purpose of a bachelor party was to engage in some debauchery for a change.

Survey Responses
Some other responses further highlight the idea of camaraderie as one of the main goals:

"To provide a Groom, his close friends, and relatives an opportunity to let it all hang out together (reminisce, tie-one-on, do things we wouldn't normally do, go places we wouldn't normally go, act like idiots without the guilt, etc.)."

"There's something different about a night that includes just men and no women. It's not all macho stuff like women think, it's hard to explain but the conversations and especially the tone of the night is just different. I like that when it happens."

"It's a chance to see old friends and/or meet new people who will be attending the wedding."

"To provide the Groom with 1) a night with his closest friends and 2) a night full of events and activities that the Groom will truly enjoy."

"A ceremony to honor friendship and to acknowledge how it changes as we go through life."

"It's a sendoff in many ways. Like a guy going off to war."

"Men also experience 'the change of life' and it begins after the bachelor party."

"The purpose of a bachelor party is a celebration of the passing of a man's singlehood into the frightening but tax friendly togetherness of holy matrimony."

"The purpose of the bachelor party is to raise funds."

What If You—the "Best Man"—Are a Woman?

Today it's not uncommon for women to be asked to be a "Best Man" or "Groomsman." From my discussions with women and men on this topic, the only real issue involves the idea of adult entertainment. My view is simple: If the Groom asked you to be part of his wedding, then he doesn't expect to be brought to a strip bar. You, a female Best Man, can bring a lot to the planning team. Your biggest handicap is that you've never attended a bachelor party. Conversely, this can be your greatest strength, because you'll be free to organize a unique event.

A female Best Man I once coached had no idea what she wanted to do for the bachelor party, but she knew she did not want to abdicate her Best Man responsibilities to the Groomsmen. After taking the survey, she realized she wanted to organize a traditional party that the men would enjoy. To this end, we organized a night that started with pool and food in a private room at a local billiards hall. The group then went

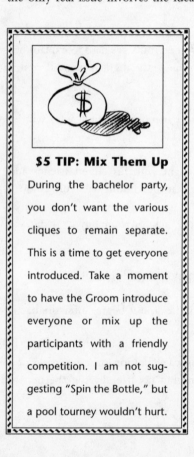

$5 TIP: Mix Them Up

During the bachelor party, you don't want the various cliques to remain separate. This is a time to get everyone introduced. Take a moment to have the Groom introduce everyone or mix up the participants with a friendly competition. I am not suggesting "Spin the Bottle," but a pool tourney wouldn't hurt.

down the street to see a pro baseball game. After the game, the group moved to a microbrewery a few blocks from the ballpark. This plan worked for her because people could choose to come to any one or all of the three parts of the bachelor party. She also liked the idea that each stage had food, drink, and activities while remaining safe and relatively inexpensive for all.

What Type of Party to Throw?

There are really no rules as to what type of bachelor party you should organize. It depends on what you and the group decide. The main concern of the men with whom I spoke was not to let the Groom down in front of all his friends and family.

If you include the Groom or Groomsmen in the planning, as is customary, you'll need to evaluate this "team"—the bachelor party planning team, if you will. This team's make-up will determine the type of party you throw. Let's take a good look at the Groom, the Bride, and the Groomsmen before we go any further.

The Four Groom Archetypes

Many questions will arise when first discussing the bachelor party with the Groomsmen. The first question is what type of bachelor party the Groom would prefer. To answer this question, you need to determine what kind of Groom you're talking about. We all go through phases in life, and the different Groomsmen may represent these different times. Does the bachelor party appeal to the high school jock, the college Deadhead, or the current corporate ladder climber?

From my experience, there are four main types of Grooms. There may be various mutations among these four species, but one main personality type will come through as you begin to plan. Take a look at the following list with your Groom in mind.

The Rambo Groom

Damn the torpedoes! Full speed ahead!

This Groom just wants his marching orders, and he doesn't concern himself with the details of the night. He feels he's on a "need-to-know basis," and prior to the party he needs to know only when and where you'll pick him up.

What can you say to that? He wants a full day or night of bachelor party antics. He understands that the more he knows, the more he'll have to explain later. He has faith in the group to throw a fun and safe night.

The Captain James T. Kirk Groom
Mr. Sulu, get ready to kick this party into Warp Nine!

This Groom has been around enough to know what he likes and doesn't like in a bachelor party. He may be a little older, and he doesn't like too many surprises—especially all in one night. He may also know his Best Man and Groomsmen too well to totally trust them with this much power so close to his wedding.

This Groom won't ask the Bride her opinion, but she would agree with most, if not all, of what will occur. This Groom also may be a bit of a control freak, with a tendency to overact and a weakness for scantily clad green women, but he does surround himself with competent men. Captain Kirk's friends might bicker at times during the planning process, but when the chips are down, you can tell they care.

The Peter Parker/Spiderman Groom
With great power comes great responsibility, even on the night of the bachelor party.

For this type, the Groom and Bride are both involved in the planning process, whether you know it or not, and they have a clear idea of what they do and do not want in the bachelor party. The Groom will set very clear limits from the beginning. The Groom and Bride both agree that they don't want adult entertainment, but most other ideas are fair game as long as all the guests are involved and the event is safe—and the Groom's Spider Sense will let him know if things are about to go wrong. Otherwise, excelsior!

Warning: If you plan to disregard the wishes of this type of Groom, there may be consequences for him even if he agrees to your new plans in a moment of weakness.

The Leave It to Beaver Groom
Gee whiz Wally, couldn't we all just go to the soda fountain for malt-eds instead?

There will be no bachelor party for this Groom. The Groom is very clear about this. He may ask some of his friends out for a quiet dinner and drinks, but that's it. No organized or planned events. The idea of a bachelor party makes the Beav uneasy, and he wants to get through the wedding without taking any unnecessary risks.

Match the Groom Game

Match the Groom type to the actual survey response that fits best.

1. The Rambo Groom _____
2. The James T. Kirk Groom _____
3. The Peter Parker Groom _____
4. The Leave It to Beaver Groom _____

a. "The bachelor party is where I see a lot of problems. The Groom and Bride's wishes should be respected. If the Bride has an issue with adult entertainment, then this should also be respected."
b. "If the Groom gives you artistic freedom, then so be it. Lock up the women and children."
c. "The Groom should have a say as to whether there should be a bachelor party. I'm afraid to get married because my friends have a tradition of traveling farther and getting more wild with each party. I'm the most conservative one of the group, and I'm concerned about what they may do to me. Call me a wimp, but it shouldn't be this way."
d. "The way I see it is that the Groom may have some definite ideas

If yes, how do you know?
9. Did he buy his first Doc Martens in the 1980s?

If yes, has he graduated to a nose ring or other forms of body art?
10. Is the Groom easily hypnotized?

If you answer yes to five or more of these questions, you have a Groom who can handle anything you throw at him. If not, you may want to go a little easy on him.

Assessing the Bride is far more important than most Best Men or Groomsmen realize.

Do You Include the Groom in the Planning?
The Best Man and Groomsmen may not want the Groom's opinion no matter what his type. If you're dealing with the Captain Kirk, Peter Parker, or Leave It to Beaver Groom, you may have a problem. Let's take a moment to look at the different viewpoints. Once again, I've tried to categorize, this time for the overall attitude of the Groomsmen. Do any of these sound familiar?

• The Drill Sergeant: "You're a guest at this party, Bub"

This Groomsmen faction feels traditions are important and thinks of the Groom as more of a guest than the host of the party. They feel strongly that they should set the agenda for the night and the Groom should follow along, no matter what's planned. This includes what and how much he drinks, where they go, and what they see.

in planning the party which may be helpful, such as who to invite, where to go, raffle prizes, etc. The Bride should realize that it's his party. She can express her opinions to her future husband but has no place to insist on anything. If the Groom is dead-set against adult entertainment or if you feel he may be uncomfortable, then the Groomsmen should respect that."

Answers: 1) b; 2) d; 3) a; 4) c

POP QUIZ: Assessing the Groom and His Definition of Fun
(Make a list of your responses and any other ideas that come to you as you plan the party.)

1. Does the Groom have any hobbies?
   If yes, do they include contact sports and/or weapons?
2. Does the Groom drink?
   If yes, does he define drinking as a nice glass of wine with dinner, or does he still prefer his alcohol by the pitcher?
3. Does the Groom still have a bottle opener on his key chain?
4. Does the Groom gamble?
   If so, can he play craps or baccarat like in the movies?
5. Does the Groom have his own collection of X-rated movies?
   If yes, are they in alphabetical order?
6. Does the Groom publicly rave about the luncheon special at the local strip bar?
7. Does the Groom golf?
   If yes, is he a serious golfer? (Note: If he drinks while golfing, by most standards he isn't a serious golfer, he's a serious drinker—see #2 and #3.)
8. Does the Groom wear women's underwear?

This type of Best Man or Groomsman gets along best with the Rambo Groom.

• The Politician: "We represent only the Groom's interest"

This group will let the Groom set the outside parameters of the bachelor party in order to form a consensus. But this group has its own hidden agenda, and in the end it will take back the Groom's illusory power and make the majority of the decisions.

This type of Best Man-Groomsmen pairing could work well with Captain Kirk or Peter Parker, depending on the decisions they make, but would spell certain disaster for a falsely secure Beaver.

• The Eddie Haskell: "Gee doesn't the Groom look nice today?"

This group will do whatever the Groom wants, mellow or wild, as long as the Groom is having a good time. This is a nice match for the Jim Kirk, Spidey, or Leave It to Beaver Grooms, but this group may let Rambo down.

The Percentages from the Survey
Overall, the results broke down as follows on the question of whether the Groom and/or the Bride should have a say in the planning of the bachelor party (including whether there should be adult entertainment):

Groom 70% (Yes) 30% (No)
Bride 25% (Yes) 75% (No)

Assessing the Bride
Assessing the Bride is far more important than most Best Men or Groomsmen realize. Some Brides have an open mind when it comes to bachelor parties, with a see-no-evil/hear-no-evil/speak-no-evil approach to the whole idea—while others have some strong feelings.

The concerned Bride may have formed her opinions from too many movies or stories about bachelor parties; from family, friends, old boyfriends; or even from the Groom himself. The point is that you can't assume anything, and my advice is to let the Groom be responsible for addressing her feelings. The real issue for you will surface if their ideas are in conflict. This situation happened to a friend of mine when the Groom was telling his future Bride one thing and the Groomsmen another. In the end, the Best Man took the heat for the night. In that scenario no one ends up happy.

Survey Responses: A Range of Women's Views
Here are three very different survey responses from women that sum up what appear to be the main views on this subject. Just thought you might want to get a feel for the spectrum of women's opinions.

"Some Grooms may not be comfortable with adult entertainment so they should be asked—even if in a subtle way. I don't think the Bride should be involved with the decision, but the Groom may want to consider the Bride's feelings. If the Bride trusts the Groom enough to spend the rest of her life with him, then she should trust him at his bachelor party. If the Bride insists on being involved, then she probably doesn't trust him."

"Planning for the wedding is the beginning of a life of making mutual decisions and compromises."

"I don't believe that a bachelor party is 'adult entertainment.' It's a poor way of celebrating your masculinity. It's degrading to yourself and to women."

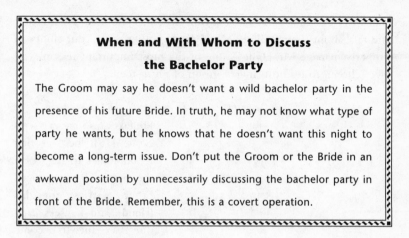

When and With Whom to Discuss the Bachelor Party

The Groom may say he doesn't want a wild bachelor party in the presence of his future Bride. In truth, he may not know what type of party he wants, but he knows that he doesn't want this night to become a long-term issue. Don't put the Groom or the Bride in an awkward position by unnecessarily discussing the bachelor party in front of the Bride. Remember, this is a covert operation.

Assessing the Groomsmen

It's important for the Best Man to realize that, for many of the Groomsmen, the time spent planning the event may be the first time they've met. How the planning goes will set the tone for their relationship throughout the wedding process. I've found that the planning of a bachelor party somehow speeds up friendships. I personally have begun many long-term friendships with other Groomsmen during this planning phase.

The Rule of Mr. Hyde

There is always one deviant in every wedding party. It's genetically encoded in all Grooms to pick at least one of his friends with the most socially unacceptable traits to represent him during the wedding process. It's like a Dr. Jekyll and Mr. Hyde phenomenon that the Best Man must attempt to control. Mr. Hyde isn't the type of guy who wants the bachelor party to be a time when all the men get together and talk about their feelings. Mr. Hyde has other plans. Your ability to properly manage Mr. Hyde is one of the most important reasons you were chosen to lead this merry group of misfit men.

"Honey, I tried to control him, but you know how _____ can be at these events."

Profile of Mr. Hyde
He takes his job very seriously. He'll be the first to volunteer to help plan the party. He's organized other parties for his friends, and he sees each one as a chance to become more creative. He'll have strong opinions about what must be included or left out. He'll be the first person to order the Groom a five-liquor-and-fruit-juice-shot, and—if you let him—he'll have the Groom's ear from that point on.

If you're dealing with a Peter Parker or Leave It to Beaver Groom, you have to control this man. If you have a Rambo or James T. Kirk Groom, you can have him do your dirty work. In the end, if the event goes well, you can take the credit, but if things go wrong, Mr. Hyde is a good scapegoat. Say this out loud as a tester: "Honey, I tried to control him, but you know how [insert Mr. Hyde's name here] can be at these events." You might think this is weak or pathetic, but file it away, just in case.

Warning: If you're the Best Man and Mr. Hyde, here are some questions to help you evaluate the overall likelihood that you'll destroy the wedding:

• Do you wish you could plan bachelor parties as a side business?
• Do you dream about the perfect bachelor party?
• Do you critique other people's bachelor parties and take notes on how to make it better?
• Do you try to "rescue" bachelor parties that you think are boring, even when you were not involved in the initial planning?
• Have you ever been referred to as a "John" by a prosecuting attorney in open court?

If you answer yes to more than three of these questions, then get professional help. And please don't ever write a book!

A Time to Punish and Embarrass

Some single guys see bachelor parties as their chance to punish the Groom for leaving their ranks. You watch—the single guys are the ones who mix the strongest and most unappealing drinks. Their goal is to increase the hangover factor by breaking the first rule everyone learns when they discover the key to their parents' liquor cabinet: Don't mix your liquor! Another reason for this abuse is that all single men know that after the wedding their friend will gravitate toward spending more time with married people (translation: the Bride's friends and not you).

Two Scenarios

Below are some true tales of bachelor party mayhem—along with some rules to follow to ensure they don't happen to you!

Scenario #1: Hijacked!

You discuss the bachelor party with the Groom, and he asks for a mellow night with the guys. You plan a night of pool and drinks, but at about eleven o'clock one of the guys who enjoys adult entertainment starts to work on the Groom about changing the plans. The Groom has had more than his normal amount to drink, and he's up for anything. So the Groom, the same guy who was so against adult entertainment and excessive drinking, is now drooling over the rail of a strip bar with fifty dollars, all in ones, in his hand. And the kicker is that you and he promised the Bride that this wouldn't happen.

Rule #1: Things change

Plans may change in the course of an evening. I've heard about this in many interviews, and I've seen it happen myself. The problem is that, because the Groom didn't want this after-hours entertainment, you didn't plan for the extra hours, the extra money, and the extra-upset Bride.

Rule #2: If he goes, you go!

This doesn't have to be a big deal, if you know enough to work it out in advance with the Groom. You're the Hannibal Smith of this A-team and you love it when a plan comes together. But in reality nothing ever happens as planned, and you don't have Mr. T backing you up. So always have a fallback strategy.

Rule #3: Dial "M" for "Mayhem"

Many Brides want Grooms to call them from the bachelor party. Often this is to make sure that the Groom has survived the night. Other times it's simply to hear his voice, because many women feel they will be able to tell from his speech whether he's drunk or he's done something stupid.

Try to persuade the Groom to promise to call her the next morning instead, and not during the actual bachelor party. If he needs to call, make sure he does so early in the evening. If this doesn't work, make arrangements for the Best Man or one of the Groomsmen to call for the Groom if he isn't well. The Bride would rather the Groom call himself, but she'll be more upset if she gets no call at all. Either way, be discreet—your male guests will see a phone call to the Bride during the bachelor party as a bad sign.

$6.25 TIP: Bankroll the Groom

Once the bachelor party has started, most Grooms don't want to think or, for that matter, remember how. This is actually one of the golden rules of bachelor parties: Grooms want to have things taken care of for them without worries. So don't be afraid to do it when it is necessary, whether it's calling a cab or calling off the last round of shots.

$10 TIP: The Safehouse

If the groom lives with his fiancée, take steps to ensure that he'll stay with someone else on the day or night of the bachelor party. If they live separately, don't listen to him when he pleads, begs and/or offers you his stereo if you drop him off at her house. This is a very bad idea. Would you want your future Bride dropped off at your house trashed and horny, reeking of cigars, alcohol, and perfume?

On second thought, don't answer that. Instead, try this one: Do you think a woman wants her future husband in this condition within a month of her wedding? Remember, women at strip bars wear enough perfume to fell a rhino at thirty paces. Any Bride will smell it a mile away.

Scenario #2: The Habeas Corpus

This situation happened to a friend of mine. After his bachelor party, he was dropped off outside his apartment—where the Bride was waiting for him—and he was a mess. He smelled like the low-end makeup counter at a large department store because of all the lap dances. He was helpless and he couldn't defend himself. Worst of all, the bachelor party was the night before the wedding, and everyone could see that the Bride was upset with him as she was walking down the aisle of the church. Not a great way to start a marriage.

Women don't accept the excuse "the guys made me drink it."

Rule #4: Take Responsibility for the Groom

The preceding problem was the Best Man's fault. Guarantee the safe conduct of the Groom to a secure location after the bachelor party. Don't put your Groom in this situation, because as a general rule women don't accept the excuse "they made me go" or "the guys made me drink it" from males over the age of ten.

When Do You Have the Bachelor Party?

It was once the tradition to have the bachelor party on the Thursday or Friday before a Saturday wedding. The proximity of the bachelor party to the wedding allowed more family and friends to be involved. It's not as common today to have the bachelor party this close to the wedding because the Friday before the wedding is now filled with longer and more elaborate rehearsals and dinners that end later in the night.

Most Grooms agree that they don't want to be hung over on their wedding day. It's now more common—and recommended—that you hold the party on a weekend night within a month of the wedding. You can't worry too much if people miss the bachelor party because they live far away; just give them a few weeks' notice and if they want to, they'll make it.

The Budget

Money is one of those subjects that makes people uncomfortable, whether it comes up among family, friends, or strangers. What makes the bachelor planning team unique is that it's often made up of members of all three of these groups. The other strange thing about money is that not everyone has the same amount, or even gives the same value to money, no matter how much they have.

I'm fully aware that what I just said was inane and just painfully obvious to everyone but the Boy in the Plastic Bubble. But the reality is you'd be amazed how many people forget these pearls of wisdom when they're planning a party. You'd also be amazed by the number of times this issue came up in the surveys and during various conversations about this book. My only advice is to take this issue into consideration and give people options on how much they want to spend.

Some Best Men or Groomsmen are uncomfortable when it comes to asking for money from the guest for events, food, and drinks. It's up to you, but most men know they will be asked for at least some money when they attend a bachelor party. Here are some answers to the question of how much money is appropriate.

• What is a reasonable price for each Groomsman to spend for hosting a bachelor party?
The range was from $25 to $200. One respondent cited "anywhere from $25 to infinity depending on the activity, financial ability, and willingness of the collective Groomsmen to chip in. It's very important to assess these factors before beginning any organizing." I couldn't have said it better myself.

• Do you think the Best Man should spend an equal, greater, or lesser amount than the Groomsmen?

70% (equal)   30% (greater)   0% (lesser)

• What normally occurs?
The Best Man pays more than the rest of the guests or the other Groomsmen!
   The Best Man should know this fact going into the planning process. If you don't want to pay for any shortfall, try to keep the costs in line with the amount of money you collect from the Groomsmen and guests. Sometimes, tickets are sold to potential guests weeks in advance of the party. This gives the Groomsmen some idea of how many people may attend, and it provides some seed money.

• What is a reasonable price for guests to spend at a bachelor party?
The range was between $25 and $75. Most men felt that asking for anything more than $100 was too much, but that each guest should have the freedom to spend as much as they wanted on the Groom.

• What is a reasonable price for transportation?
The range was between $10 and $20.

Options for Fundraising
• Pay as you go
This option allows a guest to spend as much as they want on the evening.

• One Price
I prefer the one-price-for-everything option. You ask guests to ante up once, and you don't ask them for money the rest of the night. Just make sure you don't ask for too little and leave yourself with the whole bill.

• The Big Spender Option
You can choose not to ask your guests for any money. These are the best bachelor parties. I've seen a father or a relative pick up the tab for the dinner and/or drinks at the beginning of the night. The Best Man or Groomsmen are then often only responsible for the later parts of the night.

• The Raffle
This is a popular way to raise money for the bachelor party and the Groom at the same time. A roll of tickets is bought and a prize is provided for the winner of the raffle. The extra money goes to the Groom for some spending money, and the group gets a chance to win something with the money they knew they were going to spend anyway—a win-win situation. More surveys than I expected stated that the main purpose of the bachelor party was to raise money for the Groom.

Remember, the Groom doesn't pay for anything. Even if he has more money than you do. This is a pretty firm rule—consider it a law!

Transportation

Men responded to the survey question about bachelor party transportation by listing cabs, limos, horse carriages, public transportation, private cars, and various sizes of rented vans and buses. (One respondent stated that he used camels—I'd like to hear more about that party!) You can find these and many other forms of transportation in your local yellow pages. The cost of renting a van or bus varies, depending on the size of the vehicle and whether you want to include a driver. To keep costs down for the larger group, only those guests using the van should pay for it.

$8.95 TIP: Bring a Barf Bag

This sounds silly—unless you're the person responsible for cleaning the van before it's brought back.

Another important transportation issue you need to consider is the open container law. Before you rent a vehicle for a bachelor party, find out whether your passengers can drink while you're on the road. Some states allow passengers to drink, as long as you're not sharing alcohol with the driver. You can check by calling the local police, but I wouldn't suggest asking the rental company while you're filling out their insurance forms. Also, it's a good idea to call your credit card company and your auto insurance agent to see what's covered before you pay extra for the rental company's insurance coverage.

Ideas for the Bachelor Party

The respondents were very consistent in their views about the key elements of a bachelor party.

The "Most Important" elements were:
Male Friends, Alcohol, Food, and Safe Transportation.

The "Important" elements were:
Music, Activities, and Cigars.
The "Not Important" elements were:
Co-ed Guests, Adult Entertainment, and Gambling.

One truth about bachelor parties is that there are very few rules about what you can do. The best format is to break up the event into segments that allow for natural breaks during which older guests have an opportunity to leave without feeling "inadequate." Money and imagination are your only two obstacles, but here are some ideas that may help. Use these ideas in different combinations to create a fun, memorable, and safe event.

Pool Hall

The perfect pool hall serves good food and has a private back room with one or two nice tables. This is an ideal place to start the night. It allows everyone to begin together in a location where older members of the group can meet everyone, eat, drink, play pool for a few hours, and then depart before a smaller, younger crowd leaves for its covert party mission to places unknown. Often these private rooms are only a few dollars more and can be reserved in advance. As a bonus, the pool hall will usually provide the group with their own wait staff.

The multipurpose pool hall, darts, gameroom "you-name-it-we-have-it" megaplaces are very popular now. These venues allow people with different tastes all to have fun. A problem with these locations is that people break off from the group and the camaraderie is lost. A good way to keep people together is to organize competitions with the various games.

Restaurants: A Dinner Out with the Group

I've been to a few bachelor parties where the whole group goes out for a sit-down meal. This usually works well if the group is small (less than 15). If the group is large, it's better to rent out part of a dining room and go buffet-style. This lets people move around, and it's less formal.

Gambling Venues

Living in New England has its advantages: Located within a few hours from anyplace are some of the world's largest casinos. And that's not to mention all the dog racing, horse racing, bingo, and jai alai locations. For many, Vegas is still the only place to go for the whole experience. Atlantic City is also a popular spot for much of the East Coast, despite how any one guest might personally feel about Donald Trump. FoxWoods and the Mohegan Sun in Connecticut can't build fast enough to keep up with demand. Travel agents offer some great packages to all these locations, so give them a call.

If you're going to spend time at the casino, it's a good idea to rent a van or bus and take the whole group down to the casino at one time. It's also a good idea to reserve or rent some rooms at a local hotel if the group decides they want to stay the night. Remember that the Groom will want some seed money for gambling, so factor that into your budget.

Poker Night

If the group is small, you can always start off with a little friendly game of poker. I suggest you have everyone put in the same amount to start and then have the winner buy the first round of drinks and food so it's all in good fun. Also, get some real chips. There's just no substitute for the sound they make when one is thrown on a big pile. (Then again, it could be that I just watched too many spaghetti westerns during my formative years.)

Barbecues
Fire has been used for thousands of years, and I bet it was a big hit with guys right from the start. Some anthropologists believe that within only a few weeks of the advent of fire some guy who was still trying to stand erect was already inviting his friends over to show off his new fire pit and his special Woolly Mammoth steak sauce. There's still nothing like a good group of men, a warm day, and a large number of dead animals roasting on an open fire to start a party.

One person I surveyed suggested cooking a whole pig or lamb on an open spit. I've actually been to a few of these soirees. They can last all day, and they're fun if you have someone who knows what they are doing. And don't worry about buying equipment—this is America. You can rent anything your little flame-broiling heart desires!

Bar or Pub Crawl
Picking the right location depends on the number of guests, the size and type of bars in question, and the ever-important budget. Sports bars are always a hit because of the entertainment value and the platters of good, greasy food. (Have you ever noticed how ironic it is that sports bars have twenty screens of programs highlighting the best athletes in the world, all in top physical condition, but they always serve large portions of fried food and alcohol to out-of-shape patrons? Anyway, pass the cheddar fries.)

If you intend on inviting a number of people, many bars will let you rent out a part of the bar for the first few hours of the bachelor party. This may keep the party more private and contained.

Adult Entertainment Venues

For a number of reasons, these spots are normally saved for the end of the evening. First, these bars usually have a two-drink minimum and they charge an arm and leg for each. Second, these bars are not usually known for their food—unless you like four-dollar hot dogs that have been cooking on an open turnstile for at least five hours.

Third, not everyone wants to visit these bars, especially the Bride's father. Why, you may ask? Well, would you want to watch your future son-in-law with a handful of one-dollar bills, getting accosted by naked women?

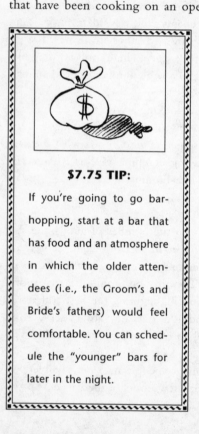

$7.75 TIP:

If you're going to go bar-hopping, start at a bar that has food and an atmosphere in which the older attendees (i.e., the Groom's and Bride's fathers) would feel comfortable. You can schedule the "younger" bars for later in the night.

Renting a Large Hotel Room

This is another popular idea. Many hotels cringe at this prospect, but what they don't know won't hurt them. The organizers of this event sometimes have the entertainment come directly to the hotel room. I've been told by some Mr. Hydes that they like to use the local yellow pages to find the best performers.

Warning: One survey respondent advised that you

choose adult entertainment very carefully. You don't want something unexpected to occur once the show begins, because once it starts there's not much you can do.

Professional Sporting Events

Some people suggested going to see a professional sporting event as a good start to a bachelor party. Have the group pick a local professional or amateur event and get a block of tickets. After the event a smaller group can always splinter off and continue the festivities.

Participatory Sports

Depending on the Groom's interests, you could start off the event at a local bowling alley, driving range, par three golfing spot, or gun range. I include the gun range in the list because my uncle who's an exceptional marksman would be upset with me for excluding his favorite hobby. I also have a 95-pound aunt from another part of the family who has a license to carry a concealed weapon, though her aim is still "unproven." I bring this up because it's in keeping with a general rule of mine: Don't piss off "good shots" or aunts wearing big jackets. This is something you might want to consider while planning the bachelor party if anyone in the Bride's family is a cartridge-carrying member of the NRA.

Sporting events are always enhanced when combined with a "round robin" tournament. The winner could get a prize associated with the sport or he could drink for free. In the surveys, some men suggested a darts competition. Call me crazy, but the combination of large amounts of alcohol and men with sharp metal throwing instruments doesn't equal fun.

Instead, I suggest sports that lend themselves to safe, healthy competition, like volleyball, ultimate Frisbee, flag football, softball, or basketball—all great group events. Just make sure the field is open for play when you need it. And you may want to check the open container laws before you unpack the coolers.

Fishing

Half-day or full-day ocean fishing trips are a blast. I've been taking charter boats since I was a kid, and it's a great day of hijinks on the high seas. I've also learned the hard way about the whole seasick thing. It's best to try to solve this problem with some good drugs (e.g., Dramamine).

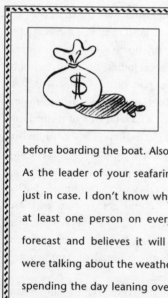

$4.99 TIP: Be Prepared for Motion Sickness

Be sure to read the directions, because you may need to take some motion sickness drugs several hours before boarding the boat. Also check to see how it reacts with alcohol. As the leader of your seafarin' crew, bring some extra doses along just in case. I don't know why, but it appears to be a tradition that at least one person on every boating trip listens to the weather forecast and believes it will be a perfect day, not realizing they were talking about the weather on land. This is the guy who ends up spending the day leaning over the railing. Don't be that guy!

Another fishing idea is to organize a freshwater trout or bass outing the morning of the bachelor party. Most men have (or at least should have) one friend or relative who freshwater fishes. A friend with a boat is an added bonus that should be exploited. This would be a great way for novices to learn to fish and for the group to get to know each other. Most serious fishermen have enough equipment collected over the years to outfit a small navy. If not, you may be able to rent everything you need from a local bait and tackle shop. There are always good stories after a fishing trip, and the best part is there are no limits to the number of times you can retell and exaggerate a fishing story.

Golfing

A popular bachelor party idea is a round of golf. Depending on the size of the group playing, it's a good idea to call ahead and speak with the pro or starter. They'll be able to get the groups off in an organized manner without making your guests wait for separate starting times.

If you want to include a greater number of the non-golfers or beginner golfers, then try a par three course or use some of the following ideas:

• Scramble ("Best Ball" Play)
Each foursome acts as one team, and the goal is to have your team end up with the lowest score at the end of the round. After each person drives, the foursome chooses one drive and picks up the other three balls. Each person then hits from the spot of the best drive. The group then picks the best second shot and, again, the other balls are picked up. Each player hits from the location of the best second shot. This works the same on the green. Depending on the skill level of the players, you can play so that each group must use at least three drives from each player during a round. This adds some strategy into the game, because you never know when someone will fall apart or get their game together for a few drives.

• Progressive
The foursome again acts like a team, and the team with the lowest final score wins. At the end of six holes each individual adds up his score. The lowest score of the group is placed on the score card. At the end of another six holes, each player adds up his score and the two lowest scores are entered on the score card. At the end of the last six holes, the lowest three scores are entered on the card. The total of these six individual scores is the total score for the team.

• Scotch Two or Scotch Four
The teams are in groups of two or four. If you're playing Scotch Two, both teammates hit off the tee. You pick the best shot and the other

person picks up their ball. The person who picked up their ball hits the ball still in play. The person who hit the drive then hits the next shot (in this case the third shot) until the ball is in the cup. You basically alternate shots with the same ball after you choose the best drive. This works the same way with Scotch Four, but with four players.

• Three Club
Each player can choose three clubs. These will be the only clubs allowed for the entire match. Some people specify that everyone has the same clubs: a driver, a putter, and a one iron. You then must hit the clubs in sequence—no matter the shot! This means that you may be putting with your driver or driving with your putter on any given hole.

• Other ideas
Longest drive: The golf pro will let you use a little stake that has a pen and pad of paper attached to it to record the name of the person who hit the shot. You place the stake off the fairway on one of the par five holes. The stake is moved to mark the location of the longest drive. The last name on the pad wins.

Closest to the pin: The pro will have a stake with a pad of paper and a tape measure that you place off the green on one of the par three holes. Each person who thinks their first shot is close can measure the shot and add his name to the pad. The person with the closest shot wins. You can also draw a circle in chalk around the pin on the same or different par three and have everyone that drives the ball into the circle win a prize.

Closest to the line: A chalk line is drawn in the middle of the fairway, lengthwise toward the green. The line starts some distance from the tee in the middle of the fairway toward the green. The length of the line depends on whether you want to reward a bad tee shot as well as a good one. A stake, with a pad attached, is placed on the spot of the closest drive to the line. The last name on the pad wins.

Golf gaming options

For more options just ask your local golf pro for assistance. They usually know all the popular games, and they've got the equipment you'll need.

Extreme Outdoor Fun

This option isn't for the testosterone-challenged. How about a white water rafting or kayaking half-day or full-day class/tour for the group? These can be organized with a guide who gives instructions—and who can save your butt when you take a bath.

Personally, I like the idea of organizing a rock-climbing class. If your group is large enough, you can hire an instructor who comes with all the equipment. These are usually half- or full-day classes that can be a lot of fun. In the same vein, there are now many rope courses available that can be rented out, again with an instructor. (A rope course consists of various obstacles that challenge participants to work together and take risks.) Your local yellow pages and/or outdoor sporting stores will have information on these and other outdoor ideas.

Paintball also gets the blood pumping. A little make-believe war can be a good group-building tool. Again, the yellow pages will have a good listing of places in your area. Sea kayaking is one of my favorite outdoor activities, and for those that haven't tried—go for it. If you're in Nebraska and reading this book, you may have to settle for a lake, or a call to your travel agent will be in order. Private tours are a great way to experience this activity.

A Night of Music for the Musical Groom

If your Groom is a musician, then a unique and fun idea could be to arrange a jam session with his band or a group of friends who play. You should be able to find some suitable practice space. This is a good example of finding an activity that your Groom is interested in and working it into the event. If the Groom is an accordion player like me, you may want to stick to pool and leave that little secret where it belongs. (For the record, I was very young at the time and I wasn't picking the instrument with girls in mind. Luckily, I stopped playing long before it had any lasting negative effects, though I still occasionally find myself humming "Lady of Spain.")

A night of live music at a local club or stadium may also be a good option for the musical groom. Try to arrange an early portion of the bachelor party, before the show, that includes the older participants.

Renting a House for a Night or Weekend
- At the Beach

One survey respondent explained that he loved the beach and water skiing. Accordingly, his Groomsmen rented a house near the beach for a weekend and they took his boat with them. The group chipped in to keep the costs down, and they had a great day of water sports. That night they had a big barbecue, and all the guests were encouraged to stay over. It was a big success.

• At a Ski Resort

There are tons of condos for rent on many of the major skiing mountains. This is a great getaway weekend for the whole group, not just the downhill skiers. Others can shop in town, cross-country ski, snowshoe, or hike. The ski lodge is also a great place to hang out and meet people. Don't be afraid to use a leg injury—try propping your leg up on a chair. (It helps if you look like you just came off the mountain, or it may help to have some ice in a bag next to you. This tactic has been used to start up a conversation since skiing was invented.) There are also some great après-ski drinking and eating bargains after a long day on the slopes.

Overnight Camping Trips

Very few people are equipped to hike into the woods for an overnight camping trip. A better idea is to organize a car camping trip that includes a day hike long enough to work up a good appetite. Most bachelor party camping trips skip the walk and focus solely on the food, drink, cigars, and campfire activities as the main entertainment. Try to bring some extra equipment for those who are not big campers, including an extra tent or sleeping bags. It's also a good idea to assign some people to bring different types of food. Include different shapes of meat and potatoes that can easily be cooked on a grill or open fire— not different types of salad, unless you're referring to pasta or potato salad. For this night or weekend you must remember that salad isn't considered "food"—salad is what "food ate when it was alive."

The Big City Adventure

To me, this option can only mean going to cities like New York, L.A., Chicago, San Francisco, and the like, where just walking around is a show in itself. If you can't find something to do in big cities like these, you should just stay home and rent a movie. Perhaps you could see *Bachelor Party* with Tom Hanks and reminisce about the roles he had to take before he won his Oscars.

The Mini Dream Vacation

Many airlines have cheap weekend getaways. A good package can include flight, hotel, and a rental car. One man told me that his four Groomsmen took him to Miami for his bachelor party on a weekend getaway. They had a great trip that they still talk about to this day. It's amazing how men can get twenty years of story mileage out of a weekend trip. These weekend trips are obviously more expensive, and are normally reserved for the Groom's inner circle (or for a Groom's second wedding). You can always organize a regular party in addition to one of these higher-cost weekend events for the Groom's other friends and family.

Cigars

Many of the men will expect cigars to be provided or available for purchase. There are now many stores, catalogs, and websites that allow you to buy cigars, so there is no excuse not to have a box ready for the group. This may be another way to raise money for the Groom. Have Mr. Hyde buy a box of good cigars and have him charge enough to cover his costs, with the extra cash going to the Groom or the Best Man to cover other costs.

Food

I can't say enough about food at bachelor parties. This is a "must have," so fit it in and give it some thought. If you're not good with grub, then ask for some help.

Major Bachelor Party Don'ts
Don't allow the use of any recording devices at the bachelor party.

The Groom should not have to worry about drunken pictures of him surfacing in the future. It's the job of the Best Man and Groomsmen to see that this doesn't happen, even if it's done in good taste or with the best of intentions. Photos at a golf match, sporting event, or barbecue are fine if the photos are taken within the first hour—not at bars, pool halls, or the like! Here's a rule of thumb for you: If it's light outside, pictures and videos are okay, but once it gets dark, they get put away.

Save the whipped cream for sundaes and the cameras for birthday parties.

One survey respondent told a story about a bachelor party that took place at a bar with a "boxing ring." Patrons could pay to wrestle with whipped-cream covered women for about ten minutes. Now, the men at this bachelor party couldn't resist entering their man into the melee, no matter what the cost. It was a mess in more ways than one. The Groom, who already had too much to drink, was thrown around the ring like a rag doll. After the "fight" he accidentally wandered into the ladies' changing room to throw up. The unamused bouncer thought he was a stalker and kicked him out of the bar without anyone from the group knowing. By this point, the group had been at the bar for

only about a half hour, and their Groom was nowhere to be found. The Best Man was concerned, to say the least. The Groom ended up talking his way back into the bar—but the whole wrestling match was captured on tape, and one guest bought a copy. This was a "no-no" because the Bride found the tape six months later, and the Groom was quite embarrassed. The moral of this story is: Save the whipped cream for sundaes and the cameras for birthday parties.

Don't play the troublemaker.

If the Groom cheats on his Bride at the bachelor party, it should be entirely his decision. Some Groomsmen make arrangements for more than just entertainment for the Groom during the course of the party. If this happens, the truth is that the Bride will eventually find out about it and your involvement. If you really are friends with this man, don't be part of something that could damage his wedding, his marriage, and his future.

What did the people surveyed have to say about bachelor party activities?

"Tattooing isn't smart."

"I had a three-day weekend retreat in the mountains. The first night we had a casual party as people rolled in. The next morning we played golf. Then we just hung out in the sun and caught up with people. That night we took a bus into town and stayed out until 6 A.M. The last day was to recover."

"If you choose to have adult entertainment, understand that its effect will only last for about a half hour until your guests lose interest. Make sure you have other things planned."

"Bad idea: the ex-girlfriend agreed to be the stripper."

"Having the bachelor party on a Sunday isn't a good idea."

Safety

You may have noticed that I've emphasized the safety issue whenever appropriate. This is because one of my relatives died in a car crash during the night of his brother's bachelor party. It's the worst thing to happen to any family—especially at a time of such joy and promise for the future. A Best Man should try to look after his guests, and if that means spending some more money on safe transportation or taking care of others when they can't think straight, do it. If you don't, you'll live to regret it, and somebody—one of the guests or an innocent bystander—might not.

What do you do if someone is drunk and wants to drive home after the bachelor party?

One time I was one of two Groomsmen planning a bachelor party for a mutual friend. The night went great, and around 2:00 A.M. we started to drop people off at their houses with the van we had rented for the night.

The last group in the van had left their cars at the Best Man's house, and some of them wanted to drive home. We were most concerned about the Bride's younger brother, because he'd been drinking and was insisting on driving home. We offered him a bed, but he wanted to sleep at his own house. We offered to drive him home—he refused. He may have been perfectly fine to drive, but we had no idea how much he'd had to drink over the course of the night. We couldn't take the risk, so we were hard on him. The Bride's brother ended up getting very upset with us for mothering him, but our greatest fear was that something would happen to him a week before his sister's wedding.

It's fair to say that the Groomsmen will be held responsible for any-thing that happens to anyone at the bachelor party. That's just the way it is, and understanding that will help in a difficult situation. In the end, the Bride's brother stayed the night, and the Bride never found out. Maybe when he reads this book, or when he's a Groomsmen and some-thing like this happens, he'll understand why we did what we did.

Chapter 3

THE REHEARSAL DINNER

THE NIGHT OF THE REHEARSAL DINNER IS A COMBINATION OF boot camp and family reunion. The actual wedding rehearsal serves as the boot camp portion of the evening because it's the last and only opportunity for instructing all the players in the ceremony about their various roles. The dinner that follows the rehearsal is often more relaxed. It allows the Bride and Groom to spend time with their inner circle and to begin the celebration of their impending nuptials. The Best Man and Groomsmen will play an integral part in this night. It's where we start to separate the men from the boys.

The Goal of the Rehearsal Dinner
Your primary goal is to learn your wedding ceremony and reception

duties. Your secondary goal is to enjoy your time with the Bride and Groom and their families before the big day.

Why Have a Rehearsal Dinner, Anyway?
When I first became involved with the wedding scene, I could never understand why everyone took the rehearsal dinner so seriously. What was the big deal? Invite some people over, say some nice words, and have some food and drink. So why do we have to practice, and why is everyone so uptight about all the small details?

This cavalier attitude dramatically altered during my own wedding. As a couple, you end up talking about your wedding day for six months to a year, and at some point you can't remember what else the two of you used to talk about or do with your time. You make more decisions in that time than you made in your life, and you hope they add up to a day your family and friends will enjoy. It turns out that the rehearsal dinner is one thing that helps minimize the stress by helping to reduce the chances of a total wedding day failure. Now I know why armies train so much—there's nothing like a real-time practice session to get everyone on the same page. If your response to this is that all weddings are the same, it's time to look closer. Although all weddings have the same goal, very few get there exactly the same way.

Part One: The Rehearsal
The first part of the rehearsal dinner night will probably begin at the site of the actual wedding ceremony. This will likely be the first time all the players are in the same place. This is an important time for the Bride and Groom because it gives them a chance to see how the people and the ceremony fit together. Expect them to want to conduct one or two actual walk-throughs of the wedding ceremony. If you're doing a

reading, you'll have a chance to walk up to the podium and get a feel for the space and the equipment. The whole rehearsal process can take some time because they'll make adjustments as they go. In the end, everyone should have a clear understanding of the order of events and their duties. This includes the Best Man and Groomsmen, so stay sharp!

$9.95 TIP: This Is No Time to Play Critic

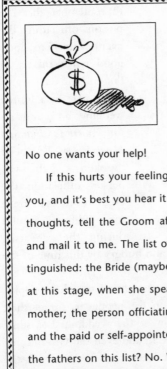

This tip is worth the price of the book. During the rehearsal, no matter how clever you think your suggestions, keep them to yourself. No one wants your help!

If this hurts your feelings, I'm sorry, but someone had to tell you, and it's best you hear it here. If you have to tell someone your thoughts, tell the Groom afterward—or better yet write it down and mail it to me. The list of cooks in this kitchen is long and distinguished: the Bride (maybe the Groom will offer his opinion, but at this stage, when she speaks, it's for both of them); the Bride's mother; the person officiating the wedding; the Groom's mother; and the paid or self-appointed family wedding planner. Do you see the fathers on this list? No. Why? BECAUSE THEY KNOW BETTER.

The rehearsal will be the first time you meet the person officiating the wedding ceremony. It's been my experience that they all run a pretty tight ship. They want the ceremony to go off without any major problems, and they know a big part of that is having everyone pay attention during the rehearsal.

It's often good to remember that the person officiating the event wants to look good when this is all done. No one wants to be part of a busted wedding and end up on *America's Funniest Home Videos*. I've been "spoken to" by the person officiating the event more than once for kidding around during the rehearsal. People start to get a little nervous, tired, and hungry by this time of the day, so patience may be in short supply.

> No one wants to be part of a busted wedding and end up on *America's Funniest Home Videos.*

The Best Man should also try to pay attention to other people's jobs at the rehearsal. It's pretty common for people to forget their duties during the confusion of the day of the wedding. For some strange reason people will ask the Best Man and even the Groomsmen for direction, so don't be surprised, and try to be ready with the right answer.

The Handshake

You'll be meeting many people during the wedding, so for those of you with bad handshakes, take this time to fix the problem. You may not even know who you are, but if you're a Groomsman, I expect you to broach this touchy subject. The soft handshake is the worst, so take hold of their hand and give it a nice shake. You may want to add a few gentle pumps or even the "two-handed" shake for added sincerity. If you get someone with a "killer grip" hand-shake, just move your hand higher toward their thumb and they can't hurt you.

The Standard Order of Events

The order of the ceremony will vary with each wedding, depending on the religion of the Bride and Groom as well as their "feel." The standard wedding begins with the procession, then an introduction by the offici-ator, a blessing or two, readings and/or songs, the exchange of wedding vows, the exchange of rings, some kisses and clapping, then a few final words of advice or encouragement. It ends with a final procession out and a receiving line, with some birdseed-throwing once the newlyweds arrive. We'll get into the specifics of all of this in the next chapter.

What If Children Are Involved in the Weddings?

Children can be a fun part of any wedding as a Ring Bearer or Flower Girl or Boy because they can add a freshness and innocence to the day that no other group can offer. It can also be a lot of work to control them during all the commotion. Depending on the kids' ages and temperaments, they can greatly increase the day's unpredictability factor.

The good news is that this is not your problem, unless any of the kids participating in the wedding are yours. A parent and/or the Bride and Groom will usually give the child any needed instruction or discipline. As a Best Man or Groomsman, I would not suggest you take on the role of disciplinarian. Let the Bride and Groom set the tone and let them deal with the child's parents if there are any problems. From my experience, kids do great at weddings because they know it is a big event, and they have fun as long as they're not asked to act like adults for too long a period.

Part Two: The Dinner

The dinner is the second and more enjoyable half of the rehearsal night. The Bride and Groom have worked out the last-minute details, and they've seen the ceremony played out live after all their months of discussion. There is very little anyone can do at this point but share some food, drink, and conversation with family and friends.

Traditionally this event will be sponsored by the Groom's parents or family. It can take place at his parent's house, or at a local restaurant, local meeting hall, country club, or hotel near the rehearsal site. These events are usually much smaller and more casual than the wedding reception because the Groom's parents know that it's bad form to steal the thunder from the Bride's parents. In recent years, rehearsal dinners have gotten larger. It used to be that only the Bride and Groom, their immediate families, and the wedding party were invited. Today, the Groom's family often invites more family, especially those who've come from out of town for the wedding.

"Honey, What Should I Wear to the Rehearsal Dinner?"
The dress code for a rehearsal dinner depends on what the Groom's parents have planned, but it'll be less formal than the wedding. I think it's a good idea (although only a suggestion) that the Best Man and Groomsmen be as dressed up—or even a little more dressed up—as the other guests. You don't have to be in your tux, but it's good to stand out a little from the group when you're a member of the wedding party.

If you're bringing a date, give your significant other a clue as to the dress code in advance. Ask the Bride what she thinks guests should wear, and also ask her what she's wearing (women never want to be more dressed up than the Bride-to-be). Trust me, big points if you have this info before your date asks you. Bigger points if, when you arrive, you were right.

"Does This Look Good?" Or: "Which Do You Like Better?"
Being a good Best Man or Groomsman is also about being a good date,
and the following advice will serve you well before the rehearsal dinner, the wedding, and hopefully for many years to come.

I know what it's like to be asked the questions: "Which one do you
like better, A or B?" or "Honey, does this make me look fat?" The key
is to respond first with a few questions before you offer your answer.
The tone of your voice is important (as always in a relationship). You're
trying to find out what her thoughts are about each one of her choices.
Ask her what she likes or dislikes about each outfit. She may explain
that one outfit is more casual or formal, or maybe she doesn't know
whether she should wear pants, a dress, a skirt, or whatever. It doesn't
matter, because she may just want to process the pros and cons of each
outfit with someone before making up her own mind.

The problem for most men is that they speak before they know
what their significant others are thinking. Others make a bigger
mistake: uttering the fateful phrase, "They both look good, honey,"
and going back to getting dressed themselves. This answer helps no
one—especially you. If she knew which one to choose, or if she had
anyone else to ask, she wouldn't be asking you. She wants feedback,
not more indecision.

Here's the rub: Once you take my advice, actually ask the right
questions, and then offer your opinion, she'll want more. Yes, in a
perfect world, a woman would be happy just to get a clear opinion
from you and then let you get dressed. In your mind, you're running
late and this whole process is just costing you more time. You may also
be wondering why she's even asking you when you're having enough
trouble dressing yourself, never mind someone else. You might also
think that if you repeatedly refuse to help her with clothing choices,

she'll eventually stop asking. All these thoughts may seem reasonable, but none is accurate. So you should be ready for her next questions: "Why do you like this one more?" or "Do you not like the other one?" or "I wear that one all the time and you've never told me you don't like it!" I may be exaggerating here, but not that much.

This is the tricky part because you're being set up. The key is to stay calm and stick to your original answer. Don't get short with her, because she wants to be dressed as much as you do. She's actually just gauging the credibility of your answer with an explanation of why you picked the one you did. It's now time to use your secret weapon—knowledge. You already know what she was thinking when she asked you.

I know, pure genius—but you're not done yet.

Try to match up your response with one of her issues. For example: "This one goes better with my outfit, and it'll look good when we are dancing together"; or "I like that color on you"; or "That's one of my favorite colors, even though I still like the other one"; or "That one's more casual, you don't want to show up the Bride"; or "You'd be more comfortable in that one, and it'll be a long night." Never admit that you don't like the other outfit, because despite your opinion, she may still wear it. You can pick any one of these answers or any combination. Just stick to your guns and it'll all be over quickly. She'll be happy that you helped without being a pain in the ass about it. It's all about the process, your tone, and some active listening.

And that's one to grow on.

Gifts

It's a tradition that the Groom gives you a gift at some time during the rehearsal dinner. The gift is a thank-you for standing up with him at the wedding. Common gifts include money clips, wrist or pocket

watches, fountain pens, tickets to a sporting event, lighters, key chains, cigar cutters, cigars, beer steins, or gift certificates to a sporting goods store or restaurant. It's nice when these gifts are engraved with the date of the wedding and your initials. The gift then becomes a nice memory of the event in later years. (The engraving also ensures that you'll keep it because it'll be harder to "re-gift" the next time you're in a jam. We'll get into that later.)

Gift Recommendations

The Best Man or Groomsmen don't customarily give the Groom a gift at the rehearsal dinner. Your wedding gift is your gift to the happy couple. If the surveys are any indication, you probably spent more than you thought you would at the bachelor party, so there's no real need to add another gift to your list.

Wedding etiquette also offers a lay-away plan. Etiquette dictates that you have up to one year from the date of the wedding to give your wedding gift without looking like a heel. Personally, the one-year rule never worked for me. I always ended up waiting nine months, and then I had no idea if I sent the couple anything. It's also embarrassing to have to ask the couple if you sent a gift because they probably don't know or care by that point. On one occasion, I mailed two or three wedding gifts at the same time after many months of torture, and within two weeks I learned that two out of three were delivered to old addresses and/or lost by the post office. My advice is to bring it with you and drop it off at the wedding.

Cash

If you give cash as a wedding gift, I am truly proud of you. As a former Groom, there's nothing like it because you can do whatever you want with it—no strings attached and no waiting in line at the returns aisle.

Unfortunately, most people don't feel comfortable giving cash because, let's face it, if you want to spend less than $100 bucks, you can't really give cash. You have to get a gift that looks like it might be worth a hundred. You can also get them a few gifts so it'll definitely look like you went all out and hit the $100 mark.

If you're over seventy years old you may want to pull the U.S. Savings Bond scam. (Do senior citizens actually think anyone keeps the bond for the hundred years it takes to reach the face value?) If you ever get one of these, run down to your local bank, cash it, and go get yourself a new CD, or maybe two if you're lucky.

Here are some tried and true gift ideas that'll be well received:

A Unique Photo Album

This gift has never let me down. I suggest the handmade paper photo albums with dried flowers inlaid into the covers. These go over well. Photo albums also don't cost you an arm and a leg, and the Bride and Groom can never have enough of them. (This isn't the case with food platters.) You'll find unique photo albums at a good stationery or crafts store.

A Gift Certificate to a Nice Restaurant

Dinner out at a nice restaurant is always an excellent idea. My wife and I received a gift certificate to a great restaurant in the city and we saved it for our one-year anniversary. It turned out to be one of our most remembered gifts because it was like an extension of the wedding. (It was also sad because I knew the one-year rule was up and so were the gifts.)

Wine

A friend went to a good local wine store and asked the wine guy to pick out wine that would last until a future wedding anniversary. He chose a red wine (they last longer than white) that would be perfect in five years and another bottle that would be perfect in ten years. The wine guy helped him write a note explaining where they were made, which grapes were used, and when to open each bottle to experience it at its very best. This takes a little extra work and may cost some good cash, depending on the wine, but it goes over very well and will be something that gets good press. Hey, maybe they will even invite you over for one anniversary and share the wine with you!

The Registry

You don't have to get fancy. If it's on the registry, chances are they want it. If not, they can always return it for something else. Often the Bride and Groom receive gifts that weren't on their registry, and these gifts may never end up being used. You may even get one of these gifts for your wedding without even knowing it . . . which brings us to re-gifting.

Re-Gifting

If you're unfamiliar with this term, let me explain. Re-gifting occurs when you get a gift and then you give it as a gift to someone else.

There's actually a big controversy brewing over this practice. I've found that men are much more comfortable with re-gifting than women are. Despite my love for the concept of the "re-gift," I wouldn't suggest trying it when you're a member of the wedding party. As a regular guest, go for it. A tip: remember to check for re-gifting clues, such as ripped boxes, old cards addressed to you that are hidden in the box, or outdated items.

The Slide Show

The Maid of Honor may want to do this. I don't know why, but women love to put on slide shows at rehearsal dinners. Of course, they pick the most embarrassing pictures and leave all the flattering shots at home. This is a great chance to unearth that picture of the Groom in his bell-bottoms, disco suit, or parachute pants ensemble. Be warned: If you're a long-time friend of the Groom, you may also get stung with a nice photo from the past.

The Best Man Rehearsal Speech

Sometimes you'll be asked to say a few words at the rehearsal dinner. It can be obvious when a Best Man isn't prepared to speak twice, so be sure you know what you'd say if asked to avoid repeating yourself. Now, don't go looking in your contract and claim that you never agreed to more than one public speaking event. This is something you can do easily, and it may turn out to be a nice refresher before your big speech during the wedding reception.

The Best Man should start with the parents of the Bride and Groom and then work his way around the room.

The MC Speech Idea

It's a treat for the Groom to hear nice things about him and his Bride before they get married. Although friends and family always have nice things to say, they often don't have an opportunity publicly to express themselves. Or they save them up for a funeral, and then what good is it?

To solve this problem, I've seen a few Best Men give a nice speech and then ask others at the rehearsal dinner to share a few thoughts, observations, or stories about the Bride and Groom. The Best Man should start with the parents of the Bride and Groom and then work his way around the room. Each time this has occurred at a rehearsal dinner, it's been the most memorable part of the night. It'll surprise you to see how people can, without preparation, come up with some very witty, thoughtful, and funny stories.

Once it starts, it can last some time, so get an idea from the Bride or Groom about the schedule for the evening. If the idea doesn't go over well, you'll know it soon enough. Just take back the floor and have a few last words to share with the group before ending your talk. A simple and nice toast wishing them well would be appropriate.

How to Answer Questions
About the Bachelor Party

Have you ever seen *Bull Durham*? If not, rent it, because there is a scene where the veteran catcher has the rookie pitcher write down stock responses to any reporter's questions. With the right canned answers, the questions are irrelevant.

It's important that you know a few of these canned answers because people will want to know the sordid details of the bachelor party, even if there aren't any. Don't fall for this. This isn't the time to get into your critique of the best and worst of the local strip bar scene. You've got a wedding to put on!

Here are some sample responses:

• "We had a good time and everyone got home safe."

• "It was great because it gave us a chance to get to know each other. [Insert dramatic pause.] That's the most important thing, don't you think?"

• "It was great meeting [insert name of Groom's friend/relative]. I'd heard so much about him."

Chapter 4

THE WEDDING CEREMONY

YOU'VE NOW REACHED GAME DAY, A DAY THAT COMBINES THE intensity of the Super Bowl, the World Series, and *Family Feud*. A day that will change the Groom's life forever.

Talk about stress. Your friend, the Groom, will know stress before this day is over. No matter how cool the Groom may seem on the outside, he's a bundle of fraying nerves on the inside. You'll notice this when he gets that deer-caught-in-the-headlights-of-his-own-future look. At that moment, you'll be earning your wings, so stay sharp. In this chapter we'll give you an overview of the various pieces of the wedding ceremony, starting with the preparation time, the wedding hall, the limo, and ushering.

The Best Man's Goal in the Wedding Ceremony

Your primary goal is to keep the Groom company during this time and make sure he's where he's supposed to be. Your secondary goal is to enjoy your time with the Bride and Groom as a member of their inner circle.

The Preparation Time

There always seem to be issues that arise during the morning of the wedding when everyone is trying to get ready or tie up some last-minute details. Normally these issues are only minor inconveniences and can be easily resolved by a cool-headed person. If you're saying to yourself, "Who has a cool head the day of their wedding or the day of their child's wedding?" then you're starting to think like a Best Man or Groomsman.

The answer to this question is you, because you'll be there to help solve some of these minor emergencies and/or add some perspective. The first step is to avoid creating problems by being late or having problems with your suit or tux. Some things can't be avoided, but the key is to be prepared and organized. Remember, you're the port in this storm.

At my wedding, we had our share of concerns. About half an hour before the wedding, the person marrying us was stuck on the highway with a flat tire; my father—an avid golfer—was still at the course with an unruly golf crowd that somehow convinced him to play eighteen holes instead of the rationed nine; my Bride was having flower issues; one Bridesmaid was having ironing problems; and one Groomsman couldn't find his suit. It also looked like it was about to rain on our ceremony, which was already set up outside. For those of you who are concerned, it all worked out just fine.

The talk of the morning's preparation will inevitably come to the topic of weather. It's only normal that everyone wants the weather to be nice on the day of a wedding. This is especially true if some portion of the ceremony or reception is outside. If the weather is bad, people will get a worried look. Their look says, "I wonder if it's a sign that they'll be in for a stormy marriage." Someone will know a story about how a friend of a friend knows someone who went to a wedding that was ruined by rain, and within a year the couple was separated. You laugh, but the topic of weather will come up, and you'll get a kick out of the stories and the unmistakable look on Great-Aunt Rose's face when she sees those storm clouds rolling in.

Best Man Myth

You don't have to be married or even dating to be a good Best Man. Keep reading, and you'll be fine, because if you're prepared, it'll be over very quickly without any real problems. Trust me.

At the Wedding Hall

When you arrive at the ceremony site, be prepared for a scene not unlike NASA mission control entering the final countdown phase. The Groom may actually start hearing the countdown to the end of single life in his head, so if he seems distracted, just give him some extra attention. Good topics for discussion include reviewing the rehearsal dinner, stories about different family members you've met, or gossip about budding romances among the Groomsmen and Bridesmaids.

Bad topics include any reference to the idea that he's about to spend the rest of his life with the same woman. This is also not a good time to discuss problems with the wedding process or with people who've been difficult over the last few days. The Bride and Groom will have the "Moon of Honey" to discuss all these things. Hopefully, though, they'll be too busy doing other things.

The Wedding Day Checklist

Here are some items for your checklist:

✓ *The Ring*
Choose the pocket that you want to use for holding the ring—I suggest the right front pocket of your tux coat. Check carefully to see if there are any holes, and don't put anything else in the pocket before the ceremony. This way, when the adrenaline is flowing, you won't have to think.

✓ *Mints, Not Gum*
Have some different types of mints for yourself and the other Groomsmen. Tic-Tacs are a good choice because they're small, minty fresh, and have only one calorie. Be sure to take them out of that little plastic box or it'll sound like you've kidnapped a small mariachi band. Save your "La Bamba" for the reception, Señor Puente.

✓ *Tissues*
You never know when you'll need one. If you deep-sea fish or sail, you know that once one person starts throwing up, it moves through the boat like a brushfire. At a wedding, once one person starts crying, others are soon to follow.

✓ *Cash*

Have some extra cash in your pocket just in case the Groom needs something. There are always last-minute things to buy or people to tip on the day of the wedding.

✓ *Bathrooms*

Know where the restrooms are. This may sound silly, but for some unknown reason, when you're part of the wedding, people assume you built the place. I don't know why, but I've been asked the strangest questions as a member of the wedding party—just answer as best you can, and do it with a smile.

Not the Time for Stand-Up

Making fun of other wedding guests is so easy to do. There are always some real characters at weddings who'll be easy targets for your rapier-like wit. The hardest thing will be to not have a comment about the Bridesmaids' dresses. Especially when everyone knows they look tacky. But somebody picked them—probably the Bride—and she'll be standing right next to you, so save the stand-up routine for your try-out tape for *Star Search*.

The Limo

Most people are in limos only a few times in their lives: at their high school prom, their wedding, and at funerals. Each of these occasions is a good reason to start drinking, but try to wait until after the actual

wedding has finished. You may laugh, but I can spin you a tale about
when this rule was broken. . . .

The Story of the Non-Ushering Ushers
It was the first time I played the part of a Groomsman. I was very
impressionable and only a shadow of the man who writes this wedding
wisdom today. The confusion began when, at the end of the rehearsal,
the priest told the Groom to be ready and in the back room at least
fifteen minutes prior to the wedding ceremony.

The Groomsmen wanted to keep an eye on the Groom, so we
met him at the hotel on the day of the wedding, picked up our
tuxes, got dressed, and headed off for the church. Both sets of families
were going directly to the church, and no one knew where the
Bride was by this time. (Perhaps she was being guarded by a team of
eunuchs across the state line.) On the way to the church, one of the
Groomsmen, Mr. Hyde, decided it was a good idea to get a few cases
of beer. The Best Man looked outmatched by this Mr. Hyde and gave
no outward indication that he thought this was a bad idea. Here's the
scene: seven men in tuxes in the middle of the day in the liquor store,
getting beer and then piling back into a waiting limo. At first I thought
it was a good idea—we'd get some beer for the after-hours party. But
Mr. Hyde wanted the beer for the limo ride to the church. At this point
I started to question this decision, but I kept my mouth shut.

We parked on a side street near enough to the church to be able to
watch people arrive. Fifteen minutes prior to the beginning of the
wedding, we proceeded to park behind the church. By now a hundred
or so people were waiting within the entranceway of the church. It was
chaos. Mr. Hyde led us to the basement entrance to avoid the crowds
we had created because people were waiting for us to seat them.

The unofficial family wedding planner found us coming up the back stairs and barked out a set of orders as we popped breath mints. Mr. Hyde simply walked up to the main doors of the church and opened them; everyone proceeded to seat themselves in about five minutes. No ushering needed.

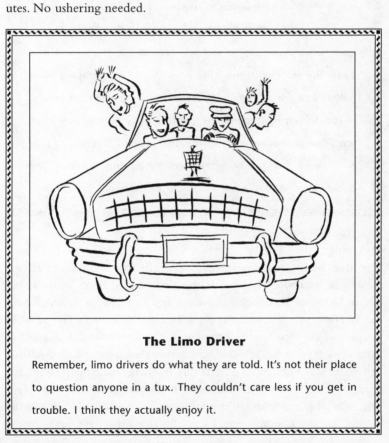

The Limo Driver

Remember, limo drivers do what they are told. It's not their place to question anyone in a tux. They couldn't care less if you get in trouble. I think they actually enjoy it.

The Wedding Planner

There is one of these at every wedding whether they are hired or not. If the Bride's family has hired a real one, give him or her some room to do what they do. You can deal with them because they know what they're doing and you can see them coming a mile away. The problem begins when a Martha Stewart wannabe starts getting into the act. Be on the lookout for a close family friend or relative who is way too into the wedding. They will take over when the Bride or mother of the Bride isn't around. This person may have some real power within the family, but not over the Groomsmen—as Best Man, that's your department.

Ushering

The Best Man doesn't normally usher. His job is to stay with the Groom in a private place while the Groomsmen greet and seat the guests. Ushering isn't rocket science, but a few tips are in order. Save the first few rows closest to the front for family members. The problem is that you may not know all the family from both sides. It's easiest to first ask each guest you're ushering whether they are guests of the Bride or Groom and whether they are family. If you're facing the podium, the Bride's guests sit on the left side and the Groom's guests sit on the right side. Seat all guests who say they are guests of both the Bride and the Groom on the Groom's side. Generally, the Bride will have invited more guests and this will even out the seating. Also, people will want to sit close to the aisle in order to take pictures.

Sometimes ushers offer their arm to each woman they usher to a seat. If the woman is accompanied by a man, he will follow a few steps behind. If there are a group of women, offer your arm to oldest women, or show them to their seats as a group. Some women like and expect this courtesy, and others just want you to seat them without all the fanfare. The Bride or the Groom may have a preference, so don't hesitate to ask their opinion.

At my sister's wedding, I ended up seating some of my brother-in-law's family in the back because I didn't know who they were. I also didn't leave enough rows near the front for all of my family. Some "big hitters" from my mother's side of the family had to sit in the back. These mistakes, no matter how innocent, should be avoided, because people have an uncanny tendency to remember a mis-seating.

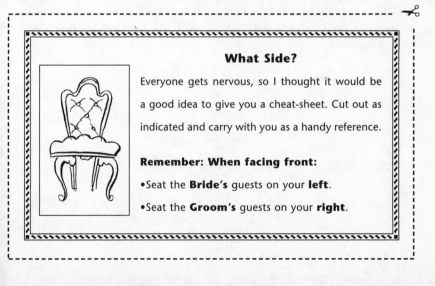

What Side?

Everyone gets nervous, so I thought it would be a good idea to give you a cheat-sheet. Cut out as indicated and carry with you as a handy reference.

Remember: When facing front:

• Seat the **Bride's** guests on your **left**.

• Seat the **Groom's** guests on your **right**.

Ushering Tips from the Survey Responses:

"When seating guests, do it as if you have been doing it all your life."

"In a hot church, seat older and heavier guests near the fans to avoid snoring or toppling."

"Don't assume the ushers know what to do. Communication is the key because they should be told what is expected of them."

"If you have a lot of people waiting to be seated, let them seat themselves."

"Be a gentleman. Guests like to feel like they're truly part of the celebration."

"Be conscientious of preset seating arrangements, and try to leave some room up front for the parents and older relatives. They often have cameras and want to be up front."

"Try not to leer at the guests while seating them . . . or at least don't get caught."

Some women's views:

"Don't insist on walking all the women down the aisle."

"Ushering is awkward. I prefer to walk with the person I came with."

"Don't walk too fast, and keep your other hand by your side."

During the Wedding Ceremony

Once the Groom and the Groomsmen are in their places and the ceremony starts, your job is to stand up there and look good. Remember, everyone will be looking at you, so no picking your nose. This may be hard for some people. Everyone gets nervous, including you, and this makes people forget things. Before the wedding, take a moment with the Groom or Bride to review the schedule. You'll also need to know the other Groomsmen's duties. Each role may be slightly different, and you may have to pinch-hit if something goes wrong. During the ceremony, remember the following:

• No leering at the Bridesmaids.

• If you're "happily single," don't gaze at any of the single Bridesmaids during the exchanging of vows. This will be perceived as your desire to be the one getting married. They will be in an altered state at this time—pun intended—so don't play with fire. This isn't flirting:

Don't Fall for It!

One trick that women play on the Best Man and Groomsmen involves painting messages like "No Fear" or "I'm Next" on the bottom of the men's shoes. When the men kneel at the altar during a Catholic Mass, the undersides of their shoes are exposed to the entire crowd, revealing the message. It's good for a laugh, but it's at your expense—so keep your shoes secure before the ceremony!

It's bachelor suicide. The real flirting can wait until later in the day. Note: Statistics say that a high number of people meet their future mates at other people's weddings. Statistics may lie, but I don't. This isn't something you want to mess with.

• Stand up straight.

• Don't lock you knees: It's not good form to faint during the ceremony.

If you're nervous, take some deep breaths and remember that you're not the one getting married.

• Again, no picking—no matter how subtle you think you're being.

• No extraneous talking: it looks like you're talking about someone. Everyone's a little self-conscious on this day—keep that in mind.

• No chewing gum or tobacco.

• Attempt to remain still. You shouldn't be unnecessarily drawing attention to yourself.

• Try to keep your hands by your side or behind you, but never in your pockets.

• Smile.

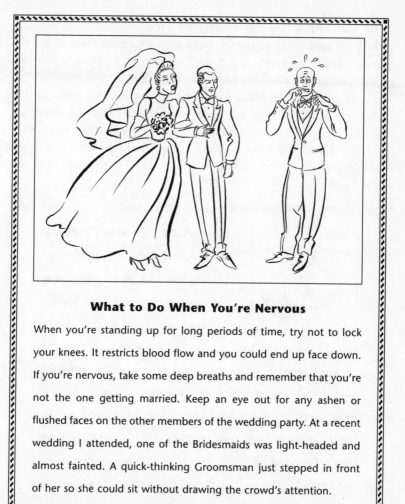

What to Do When You're Nervous

When you're standing up for long periods of time, try not to lock your knees. It restricts blood flow and you could end up face down. If you're nervous, take some deep breaths and remember that you're not the one getting married. Keep an eye out for any ashen or flushed faces on the other members of the wedding party. At a recent wedding I attended, one of the Bridesmaids was light-headed and almost fainted. A quick-thinking Groomsman just stepped in front of her so she could sit without drawing the crowd's attention.

The Procession and the Receiving Line

The procession is one of the most-photographed moments of the wedding, so take your time going down the aisle. It's like being at the pool when you were a kid—No Running! Try to look up—there aren't any holes in the floor. The only tricky part is the runner. (A runner is a thin white cloth that is rolled out right before the Bride walks down the aisle). If there's a runner, you'll need to lift your feet when you walk.

By the way, does anyone actually like patent leather shoes? Why are they so uncomfortable? It's like walking around with Tupperware on your feet!

$1.25 Tip: Bring Tissues

Try not to offer anyone the handkerchief that is in your outside jacket pocket. That one is for show only. Also avoid passing out the handkerchief in your back pocket. That one is for private use only. No one in their right mind would accept it, and do you really want it back after they're done? Let's face it—even if you wash those things, the stains never really come out. I can't wait for a laundry detergent that takes on those tough stains to be advertised on national television. That kind of cleaning power would make me a lifetime user. Until then, bring along a few tissues.

Safety During the Wedding Ceremony

Don't attempt to fix the Bride's wedding dress—ever! This isn't your job, and any attempt to help may be met with the loss of blood. This is the Maid of Honor's job. I saw a bootlegged copy of a Maid of Honor handbook that all but demanded an immediate counterstrike for this type of behavior. So don't touch that train, no matter how crumpled, unless you're ready for Armageddon.

Many weddings have a receiving line because it allows the guests a moment to congratulate the Bride, the Groom, and their families following the ceremony. For the Bride, the Groom, and their families, it's a time to meet officially and greet each of their guests before the reception begins. On rare occasions, you may be asked to stand in the receiving line. If so, receive. Smile, hug, agree that the Bride looks beautiful, and thank people for coming.

Once all the guests have gone through the receiving line, the Bride and Groom will often walk past their guests in what looks like a wedding gauntlet. As they make their way past, the guests often shower them with birdseed and good wishes. Some couples save the birdseed thing for when they leave for their honeymoon. If anyone asks, the reason no one throws rice anymore is because the birds ate the rice and quickly met their demise. As no one wants the demise of Tweety on their conscience, birdseed is now in (or for the Lawrence Welk fans, bubbles).

The Ring

Losing the ring is the ultimate no-no. I know wedding movies like *Four Weddings and a Funeral* or TV shows like *Gilligan's Island* (the episode where the Howells get remarried) come up with fun and inventive ways to solve the problem of the Best Man forgetting or losing the ring during the ceremony. But in real life, this doesn't happen.

Normally, losing the ring isn't a problem because the Best Man is so neurotic about possibly losing it that he checks on it every two seconds. Don't put it on your finger for safe-keeping. You may not be able to get it off after your hands swell because of heat and nerves. If you do lose it, the only consolation I can offer is that many Grooms lose the ring within the first few years of marriage anyway.

What Do You Do If the Groom Pulls a No-Show?

Every year there's at least one story about a Groom who pulls a no-show on the day of his wedding. If this happens when you're the Best Man, your luck sucks. And so will the next twenty-four hours of your life.

First, organize a search party using only men from the Groom's side. Don't use women, because they'll want to hurt him, and don't use men from the Bride's side, because they'll bring him home slung over the saddle of a horse like in the old westerns.

Places to look include:
- At his old girlfriends' houses
- At his mother's house
- At the airport, train, or bus terminal
- At his therapist's office
- At any bars open at 12:00 noon on a Saturday

What to do and say when you find him.
First, don't corner him like a caged animal. If you find him at a bar, buy him another drink and get one for yourself while you're at it. Your only questions for him are whether he's okay and what he wants you to say to the Bride.

Yes, you're the one who will have to break it to the Bride or one of her family members. The Bride may be distraught by this time and you may not be able to see or speak with her. She'll be guarded by the many women within her inner circle who will look at you as if they expected this to happen all along. Yes, you lucky chap, you'll be faced with dealing with her father or any and all males on her side of the family.

Warning: You're at great risk of bodily harm at this point, because all these men believe, through custom and instinct, that the Best Man is to blame. The most likely aggressor will be the father of the Bride. Watch him for any signs of quick movements. Remember, the father of the Bride is the most dangerous because he'll have to deal with the fallout of this disaster for at least a year, maybe two, making his life a living hell. In addition, he just paid for a wedding that will never happen. The need for diplomacy is an understatement. So if you can lie, now is the time to do it. Always look him in the eye, and whatever you do, don't ask what will happen to all that uneaten food.

The Photographer and/or the Videographer

You need to know when the wedding pictures take place. This should be reviewed at the rehearsal dinner, but be sure to ask if they forget to mention it. You don't want to be wandering around when they're waiting for you to take pictures. Traditionally, pictures are taken after the wedding, while the guests are enjoying some appetizers at the reception. It's currently a trend to take at least some of the pictures before the wedding ceremony, because people look fresher and it frees up some time after the ceremony. The Bride and Groom may also have planned to go somewhere beside the wedding hall for some or all of the pictures.

Let's take a moment to talk about the photographer and videographer. These people take their job pretty seriously. Also, they know Groomsmen are likely to give them the most trouble out of any group at the wedding. This doesn't mean you shouldn't try to have fun during the picture-taking time, even if this upsets the photographer. For some Groomsmen this is actually a favorite pastime, and in my view for good reason. Just don't sulk when they put you back in your place.

Some General Photo and Video Tips:

Do what they say. It's safe to say they've done this more times than you.

Ask for some fun shots of the Groomsmen together.

There will be some pictures taken with the Bridesmaids. Let the photographer and the Bride or Groom set the tone for these shots. After they get what they want, you can have some fun with other shots.

The Top Five No-No Words and Topics at Weddings

Whatever you do, don't mention the five words or topics below at the wedding, not even as a joke. I'm sure there are more than five, but these are some of the big ones.

5. "Engaged"

At a wedding this word has only one meaning: planning to be married. It no longer means to be a "happy or focused participant" even if you intend it to have that meaning. It's about commitment, so if you're a twenty-something male who has the six-month "this gum ran out of flavor" issue—don't use the word. This word is about marriage. So don't bandy it about at a wedding, even in jest, unless you're prepared to deal with the consequences.

4. "Affair"

This word is bad news even if used appropriately in a sentence with no reference to the Groom or the Bride (e.g., "The rehearsal dinner was a wonderful affair").

Why? Because any person—especially a Bridesmaid, or the Bride's family or friends—will consciously or subconsciously assume you have committed a Freudian slip and revealed a "Groomsman's secret." They'll assume that you, as a member of the Groom's inner circle, have attempted to warn the Bride that this has happened or will likely happen in the future. (Note: Some men overhearing this may surmise that a strong likelihood exists that the Bride and Groom will be separated soon and wait the full year before giving the gift.)

3. Critiquing Bridal Attire

Challenging the Bride's choice to wear white isn't a good idea. This

comment is bound to get you hit by someone, no matter how funny the discussion. Then again, if you want to go home alone—no matter if you came with your wife, a date, or if you were hitting on someone—this is a sure-fire way to reach your goal.

2. Names of Old Boyfriends/Girlfriends of the Bride/Groom

This is a strict No-No. Unless you know everyone at the wedding, you'll have no idea what connection a person with whom you're talking or anyone in earshot has with an old lover. There are many horror stories of discussions in bathrooms or at wedding tables that have caused more than one person problems—don't be that guy.

1. "Bachelor Party"

I can't say this enough. This topic is off-limits even between Grooms-men. This isn't the time to relive that night. Once again, you can't know everyone, and there's no reason to look for trouble. Stay focused. Remember the goals.

Chapter 5

THE RECEPTION

ALL RIGHT, YOU'RE ALMOST THERE. YOU'VE DONE A GREAT JOB up to this point. Now you just need to bring it home with a solid Best Man speech and a few graceful dances. But all your good work has only been a warm-up for the wedding reception, so don't lose focus now. In this chapter, we'll spend a good amount of time getting your speech in order and discussing the day's other events. Who knows? There may even be a spot for you in the Best Man and Groomsmen wax museum, which I hope to build with the proceeds from this book.

The Best Man Speech
The Best Man's speech is one of the few moments during the wedding when the Bride and Groom will not be the center of attention. It's a

high-profile job, and it unnerves many Best Men, but the Best Man speech is actually a great opportunity. It allows the Best Man to bring the room together in a toast to the future happiness of the newlyweds. It can also be a time for stories, jokes, and prayers.

Again, you may be saying to yourself, "That's great—but what about me? I'm the one responsible for getting up in front of all these people and making magic." At this point you may be questioning yourself, your manhood, and even the Groom's decision to pick you as his Best Man. Don't let doubts like these distract you. There's no better time to begin a dance with your demons. And you may actually enjoy it all if you've done your homework.

Although I can help lessen the fear of public speaking by helping you prepare an organized, thoughtful, and sincere speech, I can't make all your concerns magically disappear. Public speaking is one of the fears that all people seem to share, so take heart, grab a pad of paper, and start writing, Cicero! It'll all be over sooner than you think.

"A Few Drinks Will Just Loosen Me Up"

Wrong. Alcohol is a depressant—it works first to depress your common sense, then it compromises your ability to speak. These are two things you can't do without during your Best Man speech. You don't want to say or do something you'll regret later, and there's nothing worse than a slurred Best Man speech, no matter how great your sentiments.

Practice

My number one rule is to be prepared. Take some time to think about what you want to say, write it down in draft form, and practice it out loud. The repetition will give you confidence, and it'll lessen the common fear of blanking out on everything you wanted to say. The practice will also give you time to make any changes—something that can't be done once you push back your chair and stand up from the head table.

Videotape Your Practice

I'd also suggest that those of you who haven't taken a public speaking course or given many speeches make a video of yourself giving your speech. This may seem a bit much for some, but anyone who has completed this exercise will agree that it's a great learning tool. When you tape yourself you'll be amazed at the number of times you say "um" during a mental pause or the variety of previously unknown facial or body ticks you can develop while speaking in public. When watching the video, don't worry about your voice. It'll sound funny to you, but to everyone else it's actually how you sound. (Reassuring, isn't it?) Another reason to practice is the fact that your speech will probably be recorded at the wedding, so why not take the time to know what it looks and sounds like in advance?

"Preparedness," Meet "Spontaneity"

I'm always amazed when I hear a Best Man say that he wants his speech to sound "spontaneous," and therefore doesn't want to practice it. He'll argue that if he practices the speech, it'll end up sounding "stiff and boring." I think most people want to sound and appear as confident as the actors and politicians they see on TV. The reality is that actors, who are professionals at this, have weeks of practice for a five-minute scene that takes all day to shoot. And most politicians have a staff of speech writers and handlers who do nothing but work on making their bosses look good. No one expects you to be a pro, but why not try?

Don't Just Read

I do agree, however, that a speech that's poorly prepared and/or simply read out loud from a written "cheat sheet" can be hard to follow and ultimately boring. To solve this problem, don't write your speech onto your note cards word for word with the idea that you'll simply read your speech to the audience. I realize this method is the only way some people can give a speech, but the minute you start reading, you lose your audience. This is because it's very difficult to write a speech that sounds natural when read out loud.

> Try to give your speech as soon as possible so you can enjoy the rest of the reception.

Make an Outline

Writing and speaking are two very different mediums, so unless you're a radio personality who reads commercials all day, try to stick with an extended outline transposed on note cards. Outlines are best when they're just the highlights of your speech and not full sentences. Notes in this form will keep you on track with your outline without freaking you out if you vary from your original written speech. It's also difficult to be funny when you're reading because it's harder to give the words the inflections of a storyteller.

That's a good way to look at it: You're telling them a story—a story about you, your relationship to the Groom, your positive observations about the Groom and Bride as a couple, and your observation of how they possess the love and tools needed to share a full and happy life together.

This Is Not Your Time to Shine

The clock does not start ticking on your fifteen minutes of fame during the Best Man speech. You have to work that out for yourself some other time.

Remember: The wedding process isn't a time for the Best Man or the Groomsmen to shine. This is the Bride and Groom's event! You were only asked to share it with them and support them in making it a success.

When to Give Your Speech

This is really up to the couple. But if you have a say, try to give your speech as soon as possible so you can enjoy the rest of the reception. I always like it when the speech is given early in the reception but after everyone has had a chance to eat something, have a drink, and take their seats for dinner.

Have the Bride and Groom Join You

Have the Bride and Groom join you for your speech. Brides and Grooms rarely sit down during the reception because they're visiting each table to meet and greet their guests. If you ask them to join you, their presence will focus the crowd and allow the attention to remain with them as you give your speech. Their presence takes some of the heat off you, and will also permit you to talk directly to them as if in conversation. This lets you and the crowd witness their reactions. It's always nice to give the Bride and Groom a hug or kiss at the end of the speech. The audience loves this stuff, and if you think about it, that is why they came—so give them what they want!

The Classic Best Man's Speech

For your benefit, I've dissected some good and bad Best Man speeches and come up with an outline for the makings of a solid speech. First, the key to any speech is sincerity, so don't try to be someone or something you aren't—it always shows. Also, if you have any doubts about some questionable content that you want to include in your speech, refer back to the goals.

Thank the Bride's Family for the Wedding Reception
This is always a nice touch. Just say something like: "I'd like to take a

moment to thank the [insert Bride's family's name] for putting together this wonderful reception for all of us." Pause here to let people applaud them, then say: "We've all appreciated all their work, and I personally have enjoyed getting to know them over the last few days."

It makes you look humble, and it's nice for people to have an opportunity to give the Bride's parents some good feedback, even for just a moment.

Next take a moment to thank the Groom's family for the rehearsal dinner and all their work and support. You probably know them quite well, so you can say how good they've been to you over the years and that you want to take this opportunity to thank them.

Is This Thing On?

Take a moment and make sure people can hear you, because you may be the first person to use the microphone or give a speech at the reception. One trick is to have someone in the back signal you if there's a problem. I don't recommend asking the crowd because that's awkward, but watch their faces and you'll be able to tell.

Optional: If you grew up with the Groom, you may want to thank them for always having a full refrigerator or some other benefit they provided to you for being their son's friend (basketball hoop, toys, cars, or whatever—but not their unlocked liquor cabinet; see Sidebar: "Should I Say It?"). If you're close to them, you can ham it up by saying that you intend to pay them back if they can come up with a good interest rate and a reasonable monthly payment, or once you hit it big.

Some Basic Tips to Keep in Mind Once You Start

- Take your time.

- Speak slowly and clearly.

- Speak loudly enough for everyone to hear.

- Make eye contact with the audience.

- Look around the room, not just at one person or group.

- Keep it brief.

Who You Are and How You Know the Groom
It's good to follow up with this topic for a few reasons. First, you'll be nervous when you begin, so why not start with a topic you won't forget? Second, the crowd needs to know who you are. At other public speaking events, a Master of Ceremonies (MC) might introduce you and describe a little about you, your background, and why you were chosen to speak. This is probably not going to happen at the wedding (unless the DJ assumes this role) because you're the MC, so introduce yourself. Don't think that, because you know most of the people or met

them during the wedding process, this first step is unnecessary. Some people—even relatives—who attend the wedding won't know you from Adam.

This is nice time to tell a little about the Groom, especially a good story about how you met or about the time in your lives when you spent the most time together. People love to get the inside scoop—but keep it clean and complimentary, even if it's a backhanded compliment.

"The Story": How the Newlyweds Met

Most people say they like it when the Best Man tells a little story about how the couple met. Use your judgment here. If the couple met in a "Dominatrix" Internet chat room, you may want to filter that out.

A good "How They Met" story occurred at the same wedding that inspired this book. The Groom and his roommates lived in Connecticut, which has a number of pick-your-own strawberry fields that open during harvesttime in June. The group had a tradition of throwing a theme party at the end of strawberry season in which each guest was expected to bring some strawberry-related item. One of the Groom's female friends arrived early with an attractive guest. The Groom went up to greet them and asked the rookie what she'd brought. It turned out she'd brought strawberry shortcake, which happened to be the Groom's favorite dessert. He then publicly proclaimed that he would have to marry her. Now, the Groom was sober, and he'd never said or thought this phrase in the past, not even in jest. And it took him five years and many more strawberry shortcakes to give him the nerve to say it to her again. The story may be corny, but it is true, and the crowd loved it—especially the women, who mysteriously blocked out the five-year wait when they retold the story later that evening.

Something Embarrassing About the Groom (Optional)
This one's tricky and shouldn't be tried by everyone. In the movie *Four Weddings and a Funeral*, the star pulls off a risky wedding speech because of his charm and timing (and because he's the star and they wrote it that way). His bumbling co-star later tries the same type of speech and fails miserably. The difference was that the star said nothing that anyone, especially the Bride or Groom, could take personally. His co-star, however, mocked the Bride and mentioned the Groom's sex life and old girlfriends in the same sentence. Not a smart combination in any setting, let alone a wedding.

In the past, I've been asked to help Best Men make their speeches funnier. All I can say is be yourself; if it comes out funny, all the better. If not, it's at least sincere—and no one can ever fault you for that. Just try to have some "material" that could be funny if everything falls into place. It's all in the timing, so practice it and get some feedback from someone whose opinion you trust.

Ways He Has Changed Since He Met Her
This section is a nice touch. It allows the crowd (who may not have spent much time with the Bride and Groom as a couple) to learn about how they work together. Talk about the reasons you feel they're meant for each other or why you think they'll endure. A story that demonstrates this is also a good idea.

If you don't agree with the Groom's choice in a Bride, it can show during the Best Man speech. Try out the speech on a friend who understands your feelings and see if he or she can see through your veil of civility. If your true feelings are obvious, delete this section of your speech, or just watch more politicians on TV.

Finish strong with something positive about the Groom, the Bride, or the couple. Say something about how they're role models for you, or how you hope to be as happy when you get married, or how you hope to find someone who complements and completes you as well as this Bride has done for your friend. It may sound sappy now, but you wouldn't believe the positive reaction you'll get. If you're single and looking for love, this will greatly increase your odds. At least in the short term.

Should I Say It?

The key is to describe something embarrassing but not humiliating. There is a big difference. You want to make fun of the Groom in a way that only you can because you're his relative or best friend. This isn't the bachelor party, so when in doubt, leave it out.

Some clear No-Nos are:

• Making fun of the Bride. Let the Maid of Honor attempt this during her speech.

• Old girlfriend stories.

• Drug or alcohol abuse stories.

• Making fun of the Bride's friends.

• Embarrassing their parents or relatives.

• The "Time We Were Arrested" story.

"To my best friend . . ."

A Nice Tight Toast to Finish the Speech
One thing I've noticed is that Best Men never give the audience a chance to get a hold of their glasses for the toast. As you finish your speech, say something like, "And now for a final toast. Will everyone take a glass and raise it for a toast to the Bride and Groom?" Give them a few seconds to get ready, and when you see all the glasses raised, unload your simple, sincere last few words.

Something like this:

"To Bob and Mary: May they experience a long, happy, and healthy life together."

Survey Responses: The Best and Worst Toasts

Best:
"At one wedding, the Best Man made the observation that he was an Irish Best Man at a Jewish wedding giving an Armenian toast. He gave the toast in Armenian, and translated it as 'May you grow old on one pillow.'"

"To my best friend . . . I love you."

"An Irish toast:
        May your health be healthy,
        your wealth be wealthy,
        and your love be true.
        Jack and Jill Kelly—here's to you!"

Worst:
The Cynic: "Be careful—it's all down hill from here."

Hungry: "Best of luck to Mary and Bob. Let's dig into this great prime-rib!"

Boring and Generic: "Good luck in your life together. And I hope you have many babies."

Trashy: "May all their ups and downs be between the sheets."

Mixed Blessing: "May your days be filled with happiness, and with just enough tragedy to know the difference."

A Nice Introduction for the Maid of Honor
After the Best Man's speech, some Maids of Honor give a speech. She may not, however, want to speak after you dazzle the crowd. If she does have the chutzpah, the least you can do is give her a nice introduction. This will cement the crowd's understanding that you're the MC, this is your little show, and she's only a bit player.

Don't make fun of the Maid of Honor before you give up the floor. This always looks petty, and all your good work will be for naught.

The Family "Open Mike" Phenomenon (Optional)
This concept is similar to the idea of letting other guests speak during the rehearsal dinner. It isn't required of the Best Man, but when it works, it works great. It's something you can just offer up to the crowd; if no one bites, you can finish with your final toast.

Swearing During the Speech

This is a bad idea. If swearing is an integral part of your story, you may want to rethink it. The older generation that was not raised on MTV may use swear words sparingly, or at least only in private. This is a speech for the masses, not just for the few in the crowd who will get the "joke."

Some Tips on Best Man Speeches from the Survey Responses

"Focus on the couple and don't make it overly sarcastic. Try instead to add some humor as a way of setting the tone for the rest of the evening."

"Let the crowd get a feeling for the couple and not just the Groom, and let them express some of their good wishes. A good speech brings everyone together."

"Mention your friendship with the Groom and mention how much you believe the Bride and Groom belong together."

"Be short and sweet, with humor, sincerity, some emotion, and good stage presence."

"A speech should be fun, sentimental, anecdotal, language-appropriate, welcoming."

"Be short and to the point with your embarrassing comments, and overall keep it in good taste."

Survey Responses: The Best and Worst Speeches

Best:
"Boyhood friend (like a brother) spoke of how he was jealous of the Bride when she came into the picture. He ended with the joke that he now loves her more than the Groom. It was met with many laughs, as he wished them all the best."

"The Best Man spoke about the fact that he was unique because he was one of the few people in the room who knew the Bride and Groom not as individuals but only as a couple. He spoke in an appropriate way about the Groom's late mother. He gave a good ending toast."

"The Best Man described the couple as a good pizza and beer. He was the pizza and she was the beer. This went over well, but it had moments when you thought he was going to crash and burn. It turns out he's an actor and any other person with less stage presence wouldn't have pulled it off half as well."

Worst:
"Speech by the father of the Groom who was the Best Man. I expected something remotely sentimental for his only son and so did the Groom. Instead this quote sums up the tone of his speech: Those who support us we wish you well and those that don't can go to hell."

"All bad Best Men speeches have similar traits: the appearance that the Best Man doesn't want to be doing it, too short, not audible, inappropriate humor, inappropriate language, and an insincere toast that isn't funny or heartwarming."

"I spoke too long. People wanted to dance."

"The worst speeches are the ones concerning drunken weekends and spring break parties."

"The Best Man talked about the Groom's horrible ex-wife. Ouch!"

"As everybody should know, humor has to be appropriate for the setting. Nothing is more distasteful than a Best Man's speech with sexual overtones and foul language."

"I give them six months."

How Long Should the Speech Be?
The good news is that the Best Man's speech doesn't have to be very long. The surveys seem to peg the best length between one to five minutes or five to ten minutes. The speech should never be longer than ten minutes, and it's better on the shorter side. I've even heard a speech that was about ten seconds that worked.

At my sister's wedding, the Best Man delivered a speech that worked very nicely for him; he wasn't comfortable speaking in public, but he was sincere: "You sit here in the company of your friends and family, those you have shown love and respect over many years. May you both forever share that same love and respect for each other."

A Sample Best Man Speech
This is an actual Best Man's speech that was written according to this handbook's method. The couple liked it so much, they put it in their wedding album:

"First, I'd like to thank Rich for allowing me the privilege of being his Best Man. It seems to be genetically encoded in all men to choose the friend with the most socially unacceptable traits to represent him during the wedding process. Rich has proven this to be true. Even though this is the case, I'll ultimately be judged on my abilities as the Best Man, to give a heartwarming speech that prompts at least one guest here today to say, 'Oh wasn't that nice?'

"We should also give thanks to Rich and Lynn's family, as it's their day too. I've had the fortunate experience to have a second set of parents during my life and they were Mr. and Mrs. Smith. Their hospitality and kindness toward Rich's friends is legendary, and we're all appreciative of everything you've done for us. Having met Mr. and Mrs. Jones and spent some time with them, I've learned that they are no different from the Smiths. It's understandable how two such great people with such close-knit families have come to fall in love with each other.

"Getting to know Lynn over the past year has been a pleasure as well. I've never seen her without a smile on her face. She's a vivacious individual, and this appears to have rubbed off on Rich. You see, it used to be that with Rich you never knew what was going on in his head, especially when it came to relationships. Even if you pried you weren't going to get much out of him; he always wore the poker face, and his nonchalance was irritating because his buddies always wanted to know what was going on. So when Lynn started becoming a fixture with him, we started buzzing about the two of them. Then we started noticing some strange things after that. Rich and Lynn would start holding hands in public and sitting really close to each other at functions. And then we would ask Rich how things were going, and instead of changing the subject, which he would typically do, he would actually answer, 'Really good.' It was at this point we knew they were destined to be together.

"And Lynn, it's my opinion that you've done well for yourself in snapping up Rich. What Rich lacks in height and in golf skills, he more than makes up for in character. Rich is a man of unwavering principle, superior intellect, and high moral standing. He's a great man and an even better friend. To say Rich is a changed man because of Lynn would be an understatement. Myself or any other single man should hope to be as lucky as Rich and find a woman as beautiful and kind as Lynn to spend the rest of our lives with.

"At this time, I'd like to ask everyone to please stand and raise their glasses. I'd like to propose a toast to Rich and Lynn: Speaking for all your friends and family gathered here today, I'd like to bestow best wishes to you both, for health, happiness, and good fortune. This is the best day both your worlds have ever seen. Here's to your tomorrows being even better."

The First Dance

It's common for the wedding party to join the Bride and Groom for a song or two at the end of the Bride and Groom's first dance. This may also occur after the Bride's dance with her father or the Groom's dance with his mother. These are really the only times that you'll be expected to dance in front of the crowd. It can be an issue because many men don't like to dance. I've taught many men my secret dancing technique and they've put me in their wills, so it must work. (I have it on my to-do list to put together a "Learn to Dance" video for men at weddings, so let me know if this is something you'd want.)

Top Ten Wedding Pick-up Lines

There are no good pick-up lines at a wedding. There are only good ways to start a meaningful conversation with a stranger. Pick-up lines are for

---

Four Practical Jokes to Play on the Newlyweds

1. The classic joke (most often depicted on TV and in the movies) is decorating their getaway car with cans, soap, and gag signs. Just be sure the alarm is turned off before you start to play with the car.

2. Another oldie but goody is to soap their hotel room mirrors and write things with lipstick.

3. Hide their alarm clock under the bed and set it for some ridiculously early time in the morning. This is crude but effective.

4. Short sheeting the bed (also an old standard.)

---

bars; conversations are for weddings. It may seem like a small distinction, but in fact it's an important paradigm shift that must be made to be successful. If you want to keep using pick-up lines, focus on the wait staff or bar staff at the wedding and not the guests.

Karaoke

During this part of the reception, let your conscience be your guide. I was given a voice that can't survive even the filter of a high-quality Karaoke machine. But if you just saw *The Wedding Singer*, and feel you were born to sing "Fame" in front of a crowd, and this is your one shot to light up the sky like a flame, then who am I to stand in your way?

A built-in safety mechanism is that the Karaoke machine usually doesn't get warmed up until later in the evening, when most of the guests have gone home. I haven't seen many weddings in the past few years that had a Karaoke machine. Hopefully it was a fad that will soon make this paragraph obsolete.

The Worst Reception Story

The worst stories all have the same theme: A Best Man or Groomsman got drunk at or before the reception and made an ass of himself.

One story, and I do hope it was made up, won the prize: An ex-boyfriend was invited to the wedding. He still had strong feelings for the Bride, and he was hurt that she was getting married. Against his better judgment, he decided to go to the wedding. It was at a large hotel that was hosting other events at the same time. He ended up getting drunk, and his friends told him to leave. After a bathroom break and a check on his nerves, he stumbled back and stood up to interrupt the dinner with a toast. It went something like this: "I had your wife and she was the best, etc." As he was enlightening the crowd, he fell down, pulling the tablecloth with him on his way to the floor. All the guests had their mouths wide open as they tried to figure out who this guy was. It turned out he had wandered into the wrong wedding to give his farewell blessings.

The Garter Belt

What is there to say about this custom? After the Bride has thrown her bouquet to a single woman, the Groom takes the garter belt from his Bride's leg and throws it to a group of single men. The man who catches the garter then puts it on the leg of the woman who caught the Bride's bouquet.

I haven't been to many weddings that still practice this custom. There are many good reasons for this and if they are not obvious to you, then there's little I can say to help you. All I can say is, if it is part of the festivities, the Best Man has to help gather the single men. Try to keep the whole thing orderly, and dodge that garter belt like it was a live grenade.

Cultural Variations

If you're fortunate enough to be invited to a wedding that includes customs from the Bride's or Groom's culture that are different from yours, keep an open mind and join in the festivities wherever possible. Remember, your friend has asked you to join in celebrating his marriage in this way—if you show interest in their customs or traditions, the family will probably appreciate your interest and teach you everything you need to know. Below are some widely practiced cultural traditions.

African-American Weddings

A unique African-American tradition is "jumping the broom," a practice that began in the era of slavery, when marriage between slaves was illegal. Slaves would circumvent this law by having secret ceremonies in which the Bride and Groom would exchange vows, then jump over a broom that had been placed on the floor. The act symbolized their crossing into a new life and a new family. Many African-American couples commemorate this tradition today by jumping the broom at their reception.

Jewish Weddings

For those of you who haven't been, Jewish wedding ceremonies and receptions are usually very festive, with many unique practices even a goy can enjoy! Here are some of the basics:

• The Kituba

This is a traditional Jewish wedding contract, signed by the rabbi, the Bride, the Groom, and two witnesses. If you're the Best Man, you'll probably be one of the signatory witnesses.

• Hava Nagila (pronounced ha-va na-GEE-la)

A traditional song played at wedding receptions, during which the Bride, Groom, wedding party, and guests dance the hora, a folk dance that involves multiple circles of people with intertwined arms moving in alternating directions while stepping in an interweaving pattern. Don't be shy—jump on in and you'll be led.

• Chair Dances

Another dancing tradition, in which the Bride and Groom are lifted on separate chairs and moved around each other, often while they hold a handkerchief between them. It's the Groomsmen's job to lift both Bride and Groom—and often their mothers and fathers as well once the Bride and Groom are done. Take your cue from the wedding couple as to whether their parents should be lifted. And be careful—because the only thing you want to see broken at a Jewish wedding is a wine glass. L'Chayim!

Chapter 6

AFTER THE RECEPTION

The After-Hours Party

THE BRIDE AND GROOM MAY ASK YOU TO FIND A PLACE WHERE people can go and hang out after the wedding. It's a good idea to have the party organized before the wedding because you won't have time during or after. If the wedding is at a hotel, then the easiest thing is to pick a room and invite people back. Most people will go home, but those staying over will appreciate having a place to go. Get some things for people to drink, but not just alcohol, because some people will have stopped drinking by this time. You won't need to get food because most people will have had their fill at the wedding. All I can say is have fun. Your job is over for the night, and if there's no brunch the next day, you can get to work on the biggest hangover you can handle.

The Sunday Brunch

Many times there will be a Sunday brunch scheduled for everyone who has traveled to the wedding. This is a great time for the Bride and Groom to meet any guests they didn't speak with at the wedding reception. This is also a time to see friends and family who will be leaving for their trip home.

Critiquing weddings is a national pastime. This usually occurs on the drive home, but as a Groomsman take extra care to hold off on any comments unless they are complimentary. It's very common for people to discuss the wedding during the brunch. The brunch is really just an extension of the wedding event, and even though it's less formal and the deed is done, the Bride and Groom and the family still are entertaining. Remember, you can never assume you know the behind-the-scenes issues that arose and the hundreds of decisions that have been made.

Here are some ideas about how to respond to questions about the wedding:

If asked your opinion about the wedding, try something like: "The wedding was very special. I really liked the part when . . ." Bring up a moment during the wedding that you especially liked. It's a place to start a conversation when talking with a family member.

If asked your opinion about a mistake that occurred at the wedding, answer: "No one's going to remember that. They'll remember the day as a whole and that it was wonderful."

If asked to comment on someone else's criticism, you're being set up, and whatever you do, don't agree with them. I'm not being shallow here.

If the band sucked, everyone knows it, so there's no need to share it. The Bride, Groom, and parents of the Bride and Groom are very self-conscious about the aspects of the day. People carry a lot of baggage about what they wanted at their wedding, and parents have expectations about what they thought they could provide for their children. Also, parents always wish they could have done more, even if it looks like more than enough to you. This is just one of the laws of nature, so if you don't have anything nice to say, don't say it.

Final Thoughts from the Peanut Gallery

"Most important: A Groomsmen's first job is to assist, then have a good time. Make sure you're always on the lookout to help the guests so the Bride and the Groom can enjoy the event."

"Keep an eye on the Bride and Groom at all times. This is your chance to shine as a 'nice guy.' Always offer to get them drinks, food, etc. Let them know by your actions that everything is under control and taken care of."

"The Bride and Groom have to be the center of attention, and the Best Man and Groomsmen should not try to bring attention to themselves. Relax, do what is expected, and enjoy the day."

"Tolerate the formalities of the service, photos, and dinner—then party!"

"Know and honor the Groom's personality and wishes. Don't do anything to please 'the guys'—or the guests—that goes against the Groom's likes and dislikes."

"Remember that it's an honor to be asked to be a part of someone's wedding day. It's a PR job—behave, smile, and have fun!"

"Two words: Use tact. Represent the Groom in a manner he'll be proud of and in a way you'd want to be represented."

"Try to relax. Give support and be a calming influence."

"Make sure the Groomsmen are on time for the rehearsal and the wedding. The Best Man should be in charge of getting the tuxes. The Groom should not have to worry about this."

"Don't be a drunken fool. The entire wedding party is a reflection of the Bride and Groom."

A Few More Parting Words

Few are able to recognize the importance of a moment until it has passed. Being a Best Man or Groomsman is one of those times when I hope you'll savor each moment. To be "awake" during the entire wedding process will be your greatest gift to the Bride and Groom. It'll be appreciated, and it'll cement your friendship with both of them for many years to come.

I hope you're part of a successful wedding, and I hope this book has helped, in some way, to make your experience more rewarding. Please send me your stories of success, your speeches, your jokes, and your toasts, care of Running Press, at the address that appears on the copyright page. Most of all, have some fun, and remember—remain modest and calm, but always engaged, and you'll be a hit.

Now go out there and make the Groom proud!

Glossary

Adult entertainment: The chance to see naked the kind of women who would not talk to you in high school.

Barf bag: A container used to catch a semi-liquid projectile comprised of a foul-smelling mixture of poorly combined shots and nachos.

Bouquet: A mixture of flowers that is awkwardly carried around by the Bride for the better part of a day for no apparent reason. At some point in the day the Bride realizes she can't lift her arms anymore and throws this collection of now-dead flowers into a mosh pit of expectant single women, who fight for control of this magic elixir in the hope that it will mark the end of their single status.

Garter belt: A lace belt that the Bride places around her leg. The Groom is then invited to take off the belt in front of family and friends.

The goal of this ritual is to torture the Bride's father who, up to this point, has been able to fight off the visual of his "little girl" in the throes of passion with her husband. The Groom then throws this piece of his Bride's clothing to a pack of single males. The man who gets control of this belt gets publicly to place it on the leg of the new owner of the bouquet, without getting arrested.

Head table: A large and conspicuously placed table where the Bride and Groom sit with their wedding party. This location allows all the guests to view them as if they were animals at the zoo. This detached viewing is most evident when the wedding guests hit their glasses with dining utensils in order to have the Bride and Groom show public displays of affection. This will be the last time in the Bride's and Groom's adult lives when society will want to see them kiss in public.

Maid of Honor: The Best Man's chief adversary on the Bride's side.

Mr. Hyde: A member of the wedding party with the dormant gene that contains many of man's most socially unacceptable traits. The gene is activated once the man is given the job of Best Man or Groomsman. It's genetically encoded in all Grooms to pick at least one friend with this dormant gene.

Procession: The formal entrance of the wedding party at the start of the wedding. This ritual allows the guests to wink, smile, take pictures, and touch the Bride, Groom, and wedding party as they walk stiffly past. It also allows each married couple, for a brief moment in their otherwise obscure lives, to know the feeling of being famous and stalked by paparazzi.

Pub crawl: A tradition dating back to at least 400 A.D., when men would band together in small groups to hunt and gather in every drinking establishment that crossed their path. Today this experience is heightened when combined with large amounts of alcohol and slow rock ballads like Bruce Springsteen's "Thunder Road," Don McLean's "American Pie," or Lynyrd Skynyrd's "Free Bird."

Receiving line: A tradition wherein the Bride, the Groom, and their respective mothers and fathers—and sometimes the wedding party—line up to meet and greet each of the guests at the end of the wedding ceremony or the beginning of the wedding reception.

Registry: The practice in which the Bride and Groom go into stores they normally couldn't afford and pick out large amounts of stuff they would buy if they were spending other people's hard-earned money. The guest's job is to go to these stores and see what the Bride and Groom would like and then go find a sale on food platters at a no-name, out-of-state store that doesn't allow returns.

Rehearsal dinner: "Rehearsal" means to practice something enough times so that when it counts, you don't embarrass yourself. "Dinner" is when you eat food at night. So a rehearsal dinner is when you, first, practice the wedding ceremony, and then, when you are done, eat dinner. (This definition courtesy of "Hooked on Phonics" for the Best Man and Groomsmen.)

Skinny Bride Syndrome: This condition occurs when the Bride suddenly loses an unhealthy amount of weight over the few months prior to her wedding. It's believed to be caused by the Bride's subconscious realization that the Best Man and Groomsmen could easily destroy her wedding. The ailment also occurs because the wedding is one of the most-photographed moments of the Bride's life, and these photographs will provide evidence that justifies her asking the Groom for the next twenty years whether he thinks she's gained weight since their wedding day.

Slide show: A visual arts extravaganza that combines the medium of old and humiliating photographs with a blank wall or screen. The goal of this "act of love" is to amuse guests while humbling the Bride and Groom at a time when their egos have grown to unhealthy levels because of this extended period of unconditional love and support.

Sunday brunch: A morning meal, usually held on Sunday, that is filled with wonderfully prepared foods that you wish you could eat, if not for your upset stomach and hangover. The brunch is timed to end at least a half hour before you get your appetite back.

Toasts: A short combination of words at the end of a Best Man speech that creates a conditioned reaction in wedding guests to smile, clink glasses, drink in sips, and nod their heads.

Wedding party: A collection of random people from the Bride's and Groom's lives who for one day wear the same clothes and stand together for a large number of pictures.

Acknowledgments

The first person who deserves to be thanked is David Borgenicht
from Running Press, who supported this idea from its inception.
I'd like to thank my editors Brendan Cahill and Marc Frey, as well as all
the people who filled out surveys and/or spoke with me about this topic.
Without exaggeration, the surveys would not have been a success
without the help of Art Belvou and his trusted assistant Vinnie.
Paul Klehm's suggestions and editing also improved the surveys.

I'd also like to thank my family for their support and my wife
for endlessly talking and reading about Best Men and Groomsmen
without a single complaint. Steve Rodgers's help with proofing
and editing was also greatly appreciated. And how can I forget
Lou Roberts, whose Best Man speech gave me the idea for
this book, and his brother Charles, who graciously shared
the now-famous "how we met" story?

About the Author

Jim Grace is a writer, lawyer, and wedding junky. He has catered, bartended, planned, shopped for, made speeches at, participated in, and cleaned up after more than 100 nuptials. He has even exchanged his own vows. The only thing Jim hasn't done is perform the actual ceremony.

When not thinking about weddings, Jim is the director of a non-profit agency that assists artists with legal issues.

Jim lives in Boston with his wife, and yes, he has re-gifted.

About the Illustrator

David McGrievey has been a Best Man three times. His most interesting experience was at his brother's wedding. His flight was late, his luggage lost, and he had a flat tire on the way to the ceremony, causing only a slight delay. Needless to say, this book would have been a great help to David had he read it before his brother's wedding.

When David is not being a Best Man he's illustrating for clients such as the *Wall Street Journal*, the *New York Times*, *Town & Country* magazine, *Solgar Vitamin Company*, *Bloomingdale's* and *Monsanto*.

David lives in New York and owns a tuxedo.